ARCHITECTS ON DWELLING

ARCHITECTS ON DWELLING

edited by Christopher Platt

PARK BOOKS

In memory of Joanna Crotch and Mark Baines,
much missed friends, colleagues and inspirational teachers.

9 ACKNOWLEDGEMENTS
10 INTRODUCTION

SEVEN
PERSPECTIVES

ESSAYS

16 1 — HELLEN'S HOUSE
James Mitchell

132 INNOVATION AND
TRADITION
Dick van Gameren

30 2 — CORRECTIONS
Christopher Platt

140 'THE BLINDED MAN
SEES WITH HIS EARS
AND HANDS'
MODES OF DWELLING
Simon Henley

50 3 — THE WILL TO
ARTFULNESS
Miranda Webster

64 4 — ANATOMY OF
A TERRACE
Henry McKeown &
Ian Alexander

148 DWELLING – ON
LESSONS AND
PRACTICES IN
ARCHITECTURE
Graeme Hutton

82 5 — NEIGHBOURLINESS
Stacey Phillips

154 BIOGRAPHIES
156 IMAGE CREDITS
157 INDEX

94 6 — CAUSALITY AND
THE GENESIS OF
TYPOLOGY
Adrian Stewart

106 7 — THE PALAZZO,
THE KEEP AND
THE COMPENDIUM
OF A CITY
Stephen Hoey

I would like to thank the following colleagues who contributed to the preparation of this book: James Mitchell, Miranda Webster, Henry McKeown and Ian Alexander, Stacey Phillips, Adrian Stewart, Stephen Hoey, and the three external critical friends who provided the illuminating insights: Dick van Gameren, Simon Henley and Graeme Hutton.

I'm grateful to Karl-Heinz Schmitz for suggesting that I approach Park Books and to Brian Cairns and Gerard Platt for further help. The two initial research assistants who worked enthusiastically on the initial manuscript drafts with all the contributors, namely Dorotea Ottaviani and Ania Kozak, were welcome and creative collaborators.

I gratefully acknowledge the assistance from the Royal Society of Edinburgh, which supported the initial research that formed this book with an RSE Arts & Humanities Small Grant in 2016. Thank you also to Colin Kirkpatrick at the Glasgow School of Art Research Office for help and encouragement.

I would like to thank the editorial team at Park Books, especially Thomas Kramer for his confidence and belief in the project, and Lisa Schons and Sandra Doeller for their patient and collegial collaboration in the design and delivery of the final book. I would specially like to thank Ania Kozak for her sustained support and dedicated work on the final manuscript, without which the book would not have materialised.

Christopher Platt

INTRODUCTION

This introduction has been written during a prolonged stay at home in Glasgow, Scotland as a result of the UK Covid-19 restrictions on travel and social contact. This event has inadvertently placed a timely and intensified focus on this book's overarching theme, namely how we design dwellings. I'm privileged to live in a pleasant house from which I have a view of a garden and I can easily step out for some fresh air if I need a break from my work. The orientation and design of the house invites the sun's rays indoors at different times of the day and during the last 12 months I have found myself competing with the cat for the same sunny corners to relax in. I have noticed which plants and trees come into leaf before others and the sound of birdsong has never been more palpable nor more entrancing. My awareness of my domestic world has been heightened and intensified by this prolonged stay, particularly during daytime when I would previously have been somewhere else 'at work'. I know that I am privileged and am very aware that in contrast, many, many people in our world still live in conditions which are far from satisfactory and in some cases, desperately and dangerously primitive.This period therefore is a reminder to us all that the place we live in matters profoundly to our wellbeing. For architects, it is a particular reminder of the social responsibility we have as designers of the built environment and especially of our dwellings. Human beings thrive in good buildings, and nowhere more so than in the place where we lay our heads down at the end of each day.

Architecture can transform how you behave, who you think you are, and how you relate to others.

Exercises in Architecture, Simon Unwin, Routledge, 2012, p.2.

Design can also be seen as an ordered process in which specific activities are loosely organised to make decisions about changing the physical world to achieve identifiable goals.

Inquiry by Design, John Zeisel, W. W. Norton & Company, first published 1981, revised edition 2006, p.21.

← Opposite page: The privilege of a peaceful inside/outside connection.

This book is about how we design the places we inhabit and how those places inform the way we live. While most books on architecture focus on the architectural outcome itself, this book places the emphasis on how that outcome is created. In other words, we will learn something about the architectural process as well as the architectural product. Why is this important? Well, because it helps us to understand something about creative design processes and the kind of thinking processes which help architects establish and reach the architectural destinations. Crucially this book is written by the authors/designers themselves as they are in the unique position to explain how and why they design the way they do. It attempts to illuminate their initial motivations and inspirations as well as celebrate the final results.

This small group of projects explores 'dwelling' across a variety of different typologies, from the most modest of individual houses to complex multi-occupancy living structures. The contributors are not only practising architects, but also design tutors with longstanding engagements with architectural education, particularly in studio teaching. In other words, they help students learn how to design. This parallel activity is particularly important to the way they themselves think as architects and how they communicate their ideas to others. There is a special reciprocity between teaching and practising. I think that being involved in teaching has made me a better architect and, conversely, being active in practice has made me a better teacher. The act of teaching forces us to make explicit that which we sometimes practise intuitively.

In addition to those authors, three invited experts (all of whom are distinguished architect/educators) contribute further insights and wider perspectives which help position the work within a cultural context. In different ways they reveal how each architect articulates built form to stimulate and support a certain behaviour in the residents of their buildings. Rather than being preoccupied solely with formal aesthetics or personal influences, the architects of the case studies draw on a diverse range of inspirations to create places which address the fundamental dualities of everyday life such as shelter/identity, privacy/togetherness, inside/outside, individual/community in innovative and delightful ways. The resulting architecture makes for a remarkable collection of 21st-century dwellings which can be interpreted as hospitable stages upon which the occupants can fully act out their lives as individuals and families. As we look towards a future without Covid-19 type restrictions, we can perhaps see in a fresh way how vital a well-designed dwelling is. We can also recognise that to achieve that, we need thoughtful architects who know how to design well and can inspire us with ideas about dwelling.

Christopher Platt

7 July 2021, Glasgow

← Opposite page: The post-Covid domestic world: a place to work, rest and play.

SEVEN
PERSPECTIVES

1 — HELLEN'S HOUSE
James Mitchell

2 — CORRECTIONS
Christopher Platt

3 — THE WILL TO
ARTFULNESS
Miranda Webster

4 — ANATOMY OF
A TERRACE
Henry McKeown &
Ian Alexander

5 — NEIGHBOURLINESS
Stacey Phillips

6 — CAUSALITY AND
THE GENESIS OF
TYPOLOGY
Adrian Stewart

7 — THE PALAZZO,
THE KEEP AND
THE COMPENDIUM
OF A CITY
Stephen Hoey

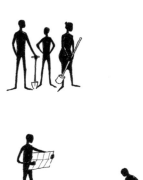

1— HELLEN'S HOUSE

James Mitchell
Orkidstudio

In the 1970s Muhammad Yunus, a young economics professor at Chittagong University in Bangladesh, began a small-scale pilot project lending tiny sums of money to poor women in neighbouring villages and townships. The purpose of these loans, many as small as a few pounds, was predominantly to provide an economic opportunity to those trapped by crushingly low salaries and who were largely ineligible for institutional facilities such as credit loans.

The theory was simple: most poor women earned an income through the production of craft goods yet the materials to produce these were provided by wealthy and often oppressive businessmen. With the sale of every chair or basket, only a pittance of profit was paid back to each woman. By keeping their producers well paid enough to stay alive but poor enough to be entirely reliant on the job, these businesses were able to retain a dependable, but exploited, taskforce.

To solve this, Yunus believed that by providing each woman with the cash equivalent to the materials for one chair or basket, she would be able to retain the full profit from each sale and then continue to purchase new supplies of materials for each subsequent product. Over time, she could then begin to expand her modest enterprise, increase her household earnings and most critically of all, have enough spare to start building savings.

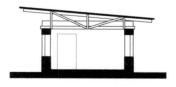

Section through Hellen's House, a simple, low-tech, structure.

From its modest beginnings, Yunus' experiment quickly found traction and in 1983 he founded the Grameen Bank. Today, Grameen operates worldwide and has spawned countless other initiatives rooted in the same simple economic theory.

Yunus' bank also proved many of its critics – arguably the majority of the world's economists at the time – wrong, as it proceeded to boast repayment rates close to 100 per cent, and far higher than any high street or commercial bank. Yunus believed that the key to this success lay in lending to women rather than men:

> Soon we saw that money going to women brought much more benefit to the family than money going to the men. So we changed our policy and gave a high priority to women. As a result, now 96% of our four million borrowers in Grameen Bank are women.

In 2013, during an Orkidstudio build in Nakuru, Kenya, a woman named Hellen Nyambura Kamau approached me for work. At this time Orkidstudio projects relied almost entirely on male labour, for no other reason than because that was the norm within the trades and construction industries in Africa and arguably elsewhere. At the time Hellen was in her late twenties and already a mother to nine children, the eldest eighteen and the youngest still a baby. The children had been fathered by two abusive and by that time deceased or estranged husbands. She earned money on a sporadic basis, lucky to even obtain two or three days work in any given week. The work was hard, ranging from hand-washing clothes for more affluent households to tilling the fields all day long. As was common, she owned no land and instead rented a rickety two-roomed timber shack barely measuring 3 × 4 m in total. For additional space her two eldest had moved in with other friends, yet the house still slept Hellen with seven young children and doubled for cooking and living functions as well.

So it was with a certain unbridled joy that Hellen accepted the job offered to her on our site. The job was offered on the same payment and terms as the male employees on site and she was charged with learning the necessary trade skills to match them by the end of the project.

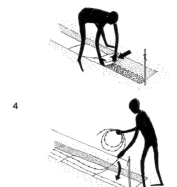

1 Setting a ground floor level
2 Excavation of foundation trenches

3 Laying a first course of earthbags
4 Barbed wire is used as a 'mortar' between each course of bags

Two of Hellen's friends work on site to build the earthbag walls.

The Nakuru Children's Home – interior

The Nakuru Children's Home – exterior

Hellen manages her repayments on the house from revenues she is able to generate by farming crops and livestock on her new land.

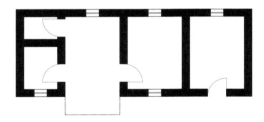

The house plan is a simple 60 m² block with two bedrooms, a living area, bathroom and store.

This particular project, for a children's home, was unique in other ways too. The primary construction method, known as 'earthbags', involved a simple system of packing woven polypropylene sacks with earth dug on site before laying them in a brickwork fashion and tamping till hard. The final wall, plastered to finish and some 400 mm thick, forming a good thermal mass for keeping internal spaces comfortable during Nakuru's hot days and cold evenings, was incredibly inexpensive and easy to replicate without skilled labour or specialist tools. As a result our work quickly gained widespread interest and recognition locally and we sought to provide training to some 60 men and women to ensure others could replicate the same techniques to build their own homes and reduce reliance on the expensive stone and cement structures which otherwise dominated the surrounding areas.

Yet a cheap building method alone was not going to solve a problem like Hellen's. In such fertile regions land prices are steep and Hellen's income, even at our favourable rate of pay, was unlikely to ever stretch that far. In short, we needed another solution.

Conscious of the founding principles of micro-finance, our first priority was not to establish a workable economic solution but instead to push the limits of what could be built at a price which was affordable even to the poorest of society.

And so it was that in March 2014, less than a year after first working with Hellen, we purchased a plot of land near her original rented house, small enough to be affordable but large enough to farm effectively, and soon set to work constructing Hellen's House. The build team was made up

1 Excavation of strip foundations.

2 A compacted gravel fill is used to drain away ground water.

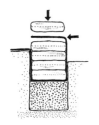

3 A waterproof layer prevents moisture rising up into the building.

4 Earthbags are used for both foundations and walls.

almost entirely of women, all close friends of Hellen, and construction was swiftly completed within five weeks.

The house cost just over £2,000, roughly one third of the cost of a comparative stone and mortar house. More encouraging still, we knew there were ways of reducing costs and improving the efficiency in both design and on-site execution. Hellen's House has since been dubbed locally as the 'warm house', with its thick earthen walls radiating the daytime heat throughout the cold nights. Our first mission was complete, proving we could build an affordable house of a quality which surpassed any local equivalents.

Our work didn't end there, however. First, we were adamant that despite our fondness for Hellen, it would set a difficult precedent to simply gift a house for free. Indeed, we felt it was more respectful of Hellen not to do so either. We therefore purchased ten chickens along with a small supply of feed and a small coup made from leftover building materials. The challenge for Hellen was to sell eggs laid by the chickens and to steadily expand her enterprise through breeding and reinvestment. Now two years on from our initial investment, Hellen has met every weekly repayment since and remains on course to repay our loan, at zero-rated interest, within a further three to four years.

With Hellen's House complete, our focus is turning towards architectural and financial models which can enable other low income earners to obtain housing, affordably and without risk. In doing this, we need to question how design and architecture can play a role in solving economic issues and in changing the means by which people can achieve security, income and shelter.

Hellen's House is now not only a means of shelter and livelihood, but a home, shaped and altered by her lifestyle. The challenge as architects or builders is to understand the hard economic issues alongside the softer aspects of place-making and comfort, and to shift our practice so that we can be agile in harnessing both.

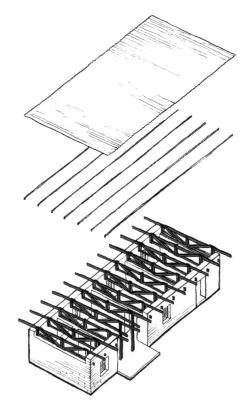

A raised 'mabati' roof is laid atop the timber structure to protect from rain and sun.

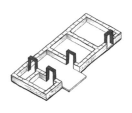

1 Door frames are inserted as the walls rise up.

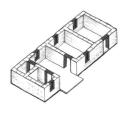

2 Window frames are added too, with the earthbags fixing them in place.

3 Timber beams are laid at ceiling height with additional earthbag courses used to hold them in place.

4 The full roof truss is built up in situ.

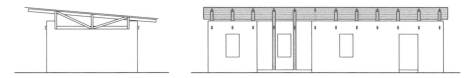

Elevations of Hellen's House show a simple single-pitch roof which shades the interior from the direct equatorial sun.

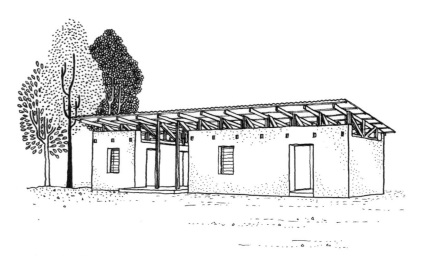

The completed home

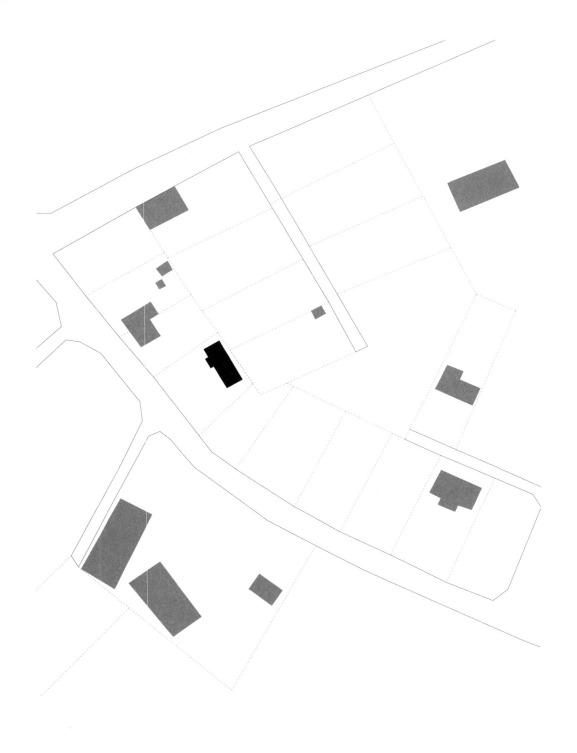

Locality plan

1

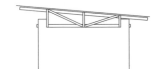

2

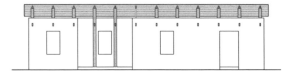

3

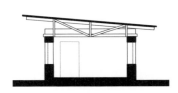

4

1 Side elevation
2 Front elevation
3 Cross section
4 Ground floor plan

0 1 2   5   10

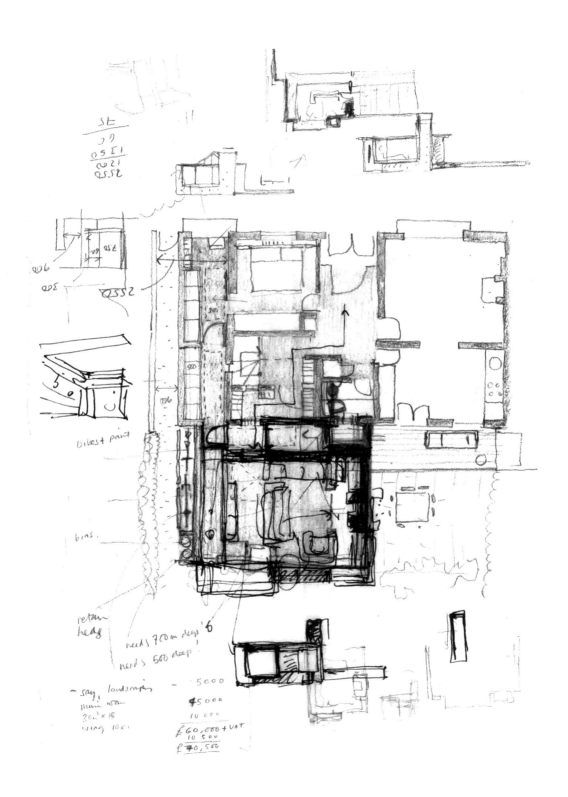

bikest point

bins.

retain
hedg

needs 700m deep 'o
needs 500 deep

~ say, landscaping — 5000
main room
30m³ x 15 $5 000
using 10 x 1   10 000
                 £ 60,000 + VAT
                 10 500
                 £ 70,500

2 — CORRECTIONS

Christopher Platt
Studio KAP

Buildings are inherently resistant to adaptation. They prefer to be built only once during their lifetime. Their structural arrangement, construction, orientation, architectural character and physical location on a site all contribute to their resistance to change. Oblivious to any shortcomings, faults or failings that have developed over time, buildings are content to remain just as they are. They appear held in suspended animation, flaunting an illusion of permanence. They are very heavy, immovable objects, up to their ankles in earth and connected by a series of underground and overground umbilical cords to centralized sources of power, water and drainage. Perhaps it's no surprise they prove so resistant to change – since they are literally stuck in the mud.

One reason a building is considered for reuse, is because it reveals its unsatisfactory characteristics to its new inhabitants. The new life to be lived within presents a fresh set of requirements which the building is invited to respond to. Rooms make life possible on the inside, suggesting that the key purpose of a building is to create an 'interior'. If architecture's role is to serve life, how should buildings adapt when life changes? How can an artefact which displays a King Canute-like obstinacy be persuaded to change its ways? This question is examined through an exploration of two domestic case studies located in the west of Scotland.

↑ The evolution of a 'settlement'
← Opposite page: Testing out ideas of the new with the old.

Major structural work is often needed in recalibrating existing buildings.

'Braefoot', in Dumgoyne, is a long, multi-extended stone cottage dating back to the 19th and, in part, 18th centuries. It has low ceilings and small windows, and is situated in an area of outstanding natural beauty half an hour's drive north of Glasgow. Its original inhabitants made their living from the surrounding land with little desire or need for views of that same landscape from within their home. Their priority was protection from the external elements in a dry and warm enclosure. By contrast, the 21st century occupants, who are not farmers, wanted to bring that external landscape into their lives in a different, direct and pleasurable manner. Their ambition was to maximize their experience of those natural surroundings by the creation of a more open inside – a stark contrast to the existing rigid spatial arrangement created by the original thick stone walls.

In the first of two phases, a new two-storey pavilion was added. This contained a kitchen/dining room and bedroom above, both exploiting the beautiful and ever-changing daylight and views outside. The existing building was reconceived as a spine which the new secondary structure was connected to, inspired in part by agricultural vernacular groupings and the nearby distillery cluster. This arrangement allowed the new additions a certain architectural freedom from the constructional and dimensional constraints of the existing building, without weakening the existing building's physical presence in the landscape. César Pelli's unbuilt Long Gallery House is a good example of a related version of the same idea. In his case, an open, glassy spine contrasts with contained, semi-independent vessels of accommodation, suggesting an intriguing future of ever-increasing spatial and formal variety.

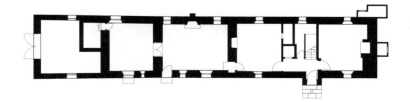

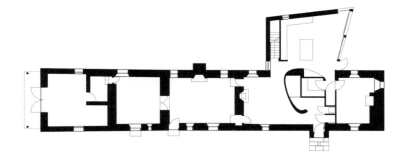

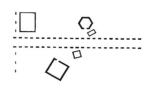

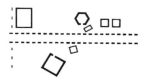

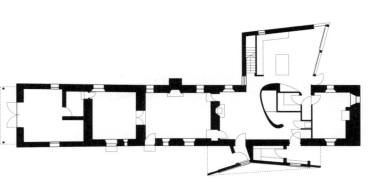

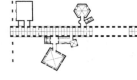

The existing plan and two subsequent phases of alterations and extension.

The growth principle.
The Long Gallery House,
C. Pelli, 1980.

The beginnings of Braefoot's transformation to the idea of 'settlement'.

Continuity of material texture and autonomy of form.

The new main entrance approach and arrival.

The second phase, created for the same client some eight years later, addressed the existing, rather abrupt main entrance sequence. Acknowledging the somewhat tangential arrival approach to the existing front door, the new structure folds and unfolds in two directions to create a welcoming and sheltered space of entrance and arrival, lightly touching the existing outer walls. Its angular, timber-clad form contrasts with the softer, rubble walls, but resonates with the first addition's non-orthogonal geometry. Both projects reinforce the memorable character of the original stone building – a seemingly permanent sculptural object in a timeless landscape setting. Both phases can be understood conceptually as autonomous, geometric structures which 'lean' against the stone spine and which also hint at the possibility of further intriguing additions over the years.

Long section/entrance elevation

Gable elevation

Cross section

Daylight enters the building in a variety of ways.

Some dwellings are constructed and others are discovered and occupied.

The 'charged' space between building and landscape becomes a convivial external terrace.

The three separate building phases at Oakley Drive, over a period of 11 years, were separate responses to the changing needs and available finances of a growing family of four. The existing building, located within a suburb of Glasgow, is one of four identical dwellings forming a generic speculative 1929 terrace of bungalows within a commercial suburban development erected by a local house builder. Phase 1 comprised essential upgrading works to the kitchen and bathroom and also linked the kitchen with the sitting and dining area to provide more open spaces conducive to attending to small children while preparing meals. Phase 2, some two years later, established a distinct children's territory within the roof space and involved the creation of two separate bedrooms, a small guest room and a bathroom. Phase 3, nine years after that, added a second sitting room with direct access to the sunny side of the garden to facilitate teenage socializing, as well as a tiny study to address an increase in adult home working. Although modest in scale, buildings of the pre-World War II period seem responsive to adaptation in ways that more distinguished pieces of architecture aren't (no ornate cornices to restore, or highly composed façades to avoid, for example). In different ways in all three phases, the internal spatial relationships were recalibrated and the indoor and the outer realms brought closer together.

These phases of alterations are very clear responses to the changing needs of privacy and sociability in a growing family. The evolution of family activities in this home has demanded a response from the very built fabric which supports those activities. At the early stages of family life, when children often require to be overseen or observed, open-plan living is useful. As children move into puberty, they and their parents have a greater need for privacy and their own territories and conse-

quently, a dwelling needs to offer a suitable spatial configuration to address those needs. Taking part in family activities in these later years is after all often a choice rather than an obligation. The family has become a mini-society in many ways, and so can be supported by 'a society of rooms' as Kahn once described.

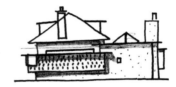

Exploring the massing connection between existing and new.

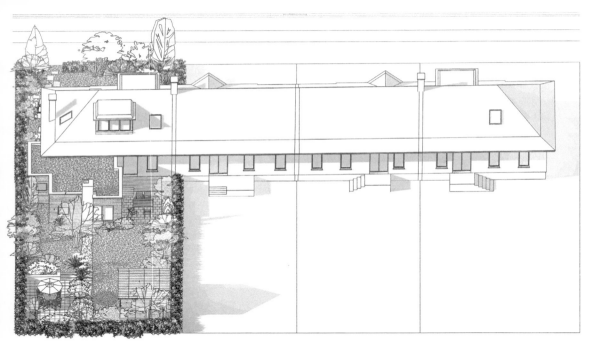

The 1929 terraced bungalow and south/west facing rear garden.

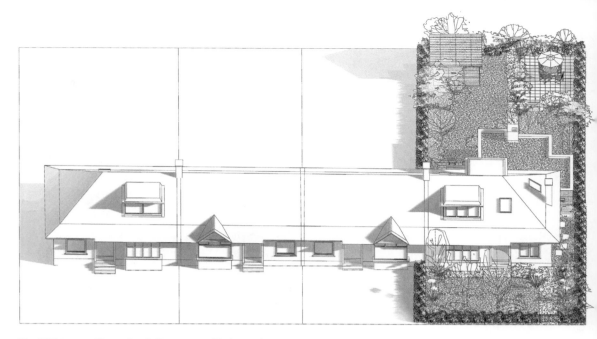

The 1929 terraced bungalow in its context with three other
neighbouring dwellings.

A bay window and a chimney define and describe the new work externally.

Studies of the bay window configuration and cedar shakes cladding.

How do we go about figuring out these things as architects? How do we broker the discussion between one (inanimate) party whose heels are firmly dug in and another (human) party which is investing money to implement the change? The simple answer lies in asking lots of questions. Firstly of our clients, and secondly of the building and wider context. We listen carefully to the responses our clients make to our questions and how they are expressed. We scrutinize the characteristics of the physical and cultural context. Of all those questions, there is one that the design solution must answer comprehensively: 'How do you want to live?' This encapsulates the underlying reason why someone chooses to undertake the often arduous task of creating, rather than purchasing, a place to live. This single question encompasses all other detailed requirements and it needs careful unpacking to inform the design process in a practical and meaningful way. Although this process of collaboration between individual client and individual architect can be very fruitful and establish a deep and effective working relationship, this kind of creative consultation is not a simple task. It is often the case that '… a couple wanting a new house is the toughest kind of client an architect can have…'.[1]

Much of our work in practice involves adjusting and recalibrating older dwellings which fall short of their owners' current and future needs and aspirations. We are asked to correct what have become inadequacies; unlocking unforeseen potential and making spatial rearrangements to create useful and pleasurable places to live in. The design process of engaging with an existing construction is very much a push and pull affair. It involves understanding the inherent spatial and structural patterns and qualities as well as inventing new ones which can address the new requirements better. It requires design insight into what needs to be reconsidered and replaced and what is best retained or conserved. 'Conservation' in this context is understood by us '…to be positive, permitting constructive and inspired change in the service of life',[2] rather than a resistance to change at all costs.

Discussions with clients show that, for those of us lucky enough to be able to influence our private domestic environment beyond basic internal decoration, we have certain particular desires for what our homes should provide.

- A desire for a more direct connection between the inside and the outside.

- A desire for a more fluid spatial connection internally between the spaces where cooking, eating and socializing take place.

- A desire for a space set apart for the family to watch screen-based entertainment (sometimes referred to as a 'snug'), often as a result of creating a more fluid spatial arrangement described above.

- A desire for practical and discreetly located places for laundry, utility and bathroom activities.

- A desire for a greater degree of daylight and sense of space.

Why is that? It is simply because these are the things that will make living in the house pleasurable; things that will make being there a delight. These wishes are not particularly original, revolutionary or unreasonable. All are on the continuum of spatial containment and openness. In the world of architectural corrections, a building acts like a reluctant patient undergoing a medical procedure, its very skin and skeleton being reconsidered, readjusted and renewed in order to frame, support a new life.

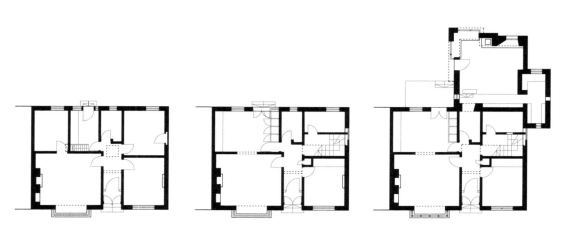

The existing plan and two phases of alterations.

The views to the garden are 'refreshed' by a variety of different window openings.

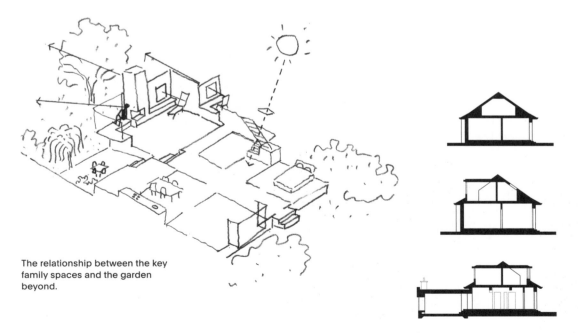

The relationship between the key family spaces and the garden beyond.

The existing section and two phases of alterations.

Working with and designing for individual families is a very different process than working on almost any other architectural commission. Firstly, with individual dwellings, most people are first-time clients, undertaking what will be in effect the single biggest financial investment of their lives. Secondly, the private client is both employer and user of the intended design; a condition rare in non-domestic commissions. Thirdly, we architects have our own everyday experience as fellow-dwellers to draw on in developing an understanding of and empathy for a client's needs and aspirations. Simply put, we help a family create their home. That's not a sentimental notion because it is something fundamental to all our existences and identities. We collaborate firstly with a family and then with a builder. We make something together which is physical and tangible and which underpins their entire lives and yet paradoxically is something which becomes more invisible the more it is used and loved. That is the transformative process by which a successful dwelling becomes a real home. The domestic surroundings are transformed from something physical but opaque to something which is enigmatic and transparent. It becomes a filter through which we concentrate on life's daily activities. Over time, we cease to consciously think about our surroundings as we once did and our home helps us to get on with our lives, as Peter Zumthor has remarked, in the way a good piece of clothing does.[3]

Our dwelling 'desires', namely shelter, light, warmth, a balance of privacy and togetherness, and contact between the inside and outside, require buildings to participate in acts of transformation. Despite different degrees of stubbornness, these two very different buildings illustrate a variety of spatial corrections and compositional adjustments which allow both buildings to be the containers of new life and in doing so extend their usefulness and meaning into the future. Architecture always exists within a predetermined physical context, be it man-made or natural. The particular characteristic of a building being both inhabitable and site specific, distinguishes architecture from other forms of three dimensional design. Those two characteristics, the one relating to human life and the other relating to the idea of place, are both inextricably linked to the problem of making inspiring and useful dwellings.

1   Kevin Roche, quoted in Thomas Weaver, 'In Conversation with Kevin Roche', in *AA Files* No. 71, 2015 (p. 44).
2   Robert Maguire, 'Conservation and Diverging Philosophies', in *Journal of Architectural Conservation* No. 1, 1997 (pp. 7–18).
3   Peter Zumthor interview, 'Different Kinds of Silence'. Louisiana Channel, 30 Nov. 2015.

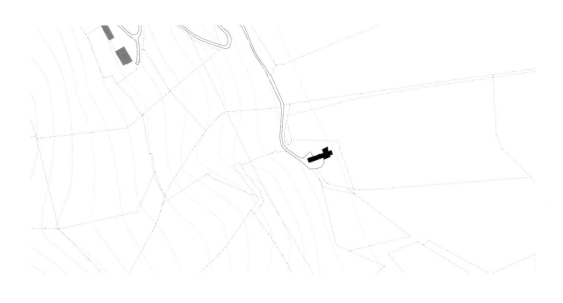

1

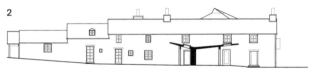

2

3

4

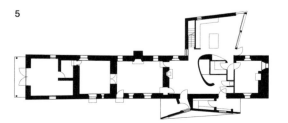

5

Braefoot:
1 front elevation
2 long section
3 side elevation
4 cross section
5 ground floor plan

0 1 2   5   10

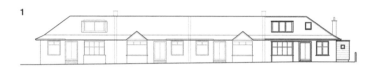

1

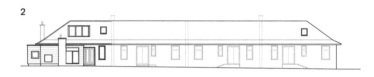

2

3

4

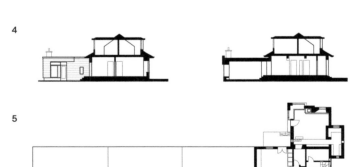

5

Oakley Drive:
1 street elevation
2 garden elevation
3 long section
4 cross sections
5 ground floor plan

0 1 2   5   10

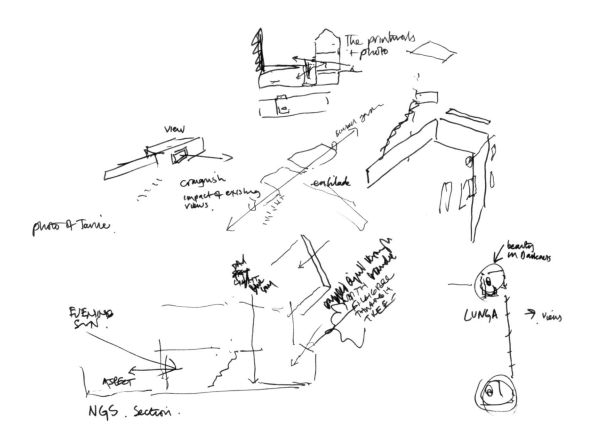

The printerals
+ photo

view

cragnish
impact of existing
views.

Buckell down

enfilade

beauty
in Darkness

photo of Janie.

EVENING
SUN.

LUNGA → views

ASPECT

NGS. Section.

3 — THE WILL TO ARTFULNESS

Miranda Webster
cameronwebster
architects

We are unavoidably steeped in the art of architecture, and are constantly adding to our knowledge and understanding of buildings and of different ways of doing things. We use a range of tools to analyse the client's needs and wishes and the qualities of the site, and wish to offer the client something extra that they had not thought of, that is beyond and better than their expectations. In listening to a client and thinking about what we might do, we have 'a will to artfulness', and are not merely knitting a design to their pattern. In some instances this might be described as formalism, and there is always a danger of settling on preconceptions that may not fit and which we wish to avoid. We have a conscious and unconscious desire to avoid overly dramatic shapes and rhetoric, admiring the Smithson's concept of 'ordinariness', and wish to arrive at a solution that may appear to be very simple but has an underlying richness.

As architects we are educated to intuitively balance a complex range of different requirements when designing, drawing subconsciously on a wide range of principles and precedents as well as attending to the client's programme and brief. Listing the principles and methods that we employ runs the risk of overlooking the less measurable and the less conscious moves we might make: there is no guarantee that such a list covers the whole story, as Alvar Aalto said:

…the large number of different demands and sub problems form an obstacle that is difficult for the architectural concept to break through. In such cases I work – sometimes totally – on instinct.

We are searching for something in a design that will somehow transcend the merely utilitarian and touch the senses in a poetic way, although we often may cloak this in a logical rationale when discussing a project with a client.

→ Following page:
Cape Cove, the shore of Loch Long.

Generally when designing in Scotland we may wish to use our artifice to create the opportunity for different lifestyles in our buildings. These may defer to the Scottish climate in some respects, but also create additional and more unexpected results. These can be achieved by thinking imaginatively about how the spaces feel, for example in considering how the soft Scottish daylight is introduced internally, and how sunlight can be modulated, such as in the high-level glazing in our inner city backlands project at North Gardiner Street, where privacy and being overlooked were added constraints.

There will be a need for a range of different spaces, some that allow for a comfortable feeling of shelter and a cosy intimacy: perhaps seeking beauty in darkness.

For the spectacular site at Lunga we have tried to contrast the sunny glazed living area with darker spaces leading into it and at the edges. The other larger and more open space here has a different physiological impact, invoking a more relaxed Mediterranean lifestyle, as well as being sufficient perhaps to dance "Strip the Willow" in a suitably energetic fashion.

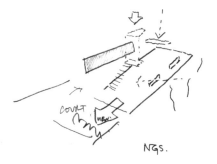

North Gardner Street: plan organization.

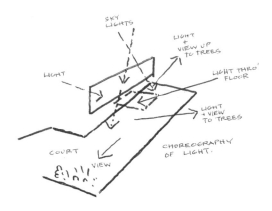

North Gardner Street: light and view
The reconfiguration of a disused furniture workshop, within a back court of an urban block. Bringing light into the deep plan was a priority, while retaining privacy and allowing key views.

North Gardner Street: section through house front to back.

1 Front garden
2 Kitchen
3 Living Room
4 Bedroom
5 Hall
6 Master Bedroom
7 Loft storage
8 Loft room
9 Terrace

→ Opposite page: North Gardner Street House
   Light well, looking up from ground floor.

54

House at Lunga
View North from living room.

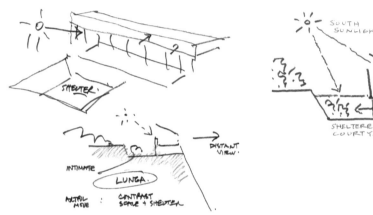

House at Lunga
Captures south light while addressing
views to the north.

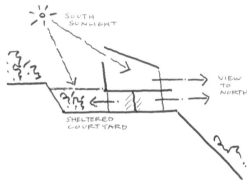

House at Lunga
Microclimates

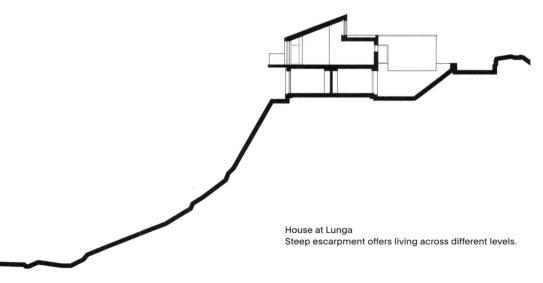

House at Lunga
Steep escarpment offers living across different levels.

Craignish
Living room peeps over rocks
catching north and west
light and views.

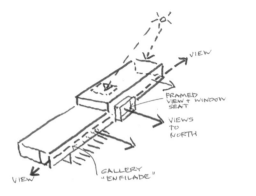

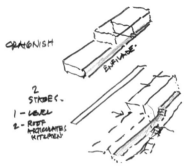

Craignish
The journey through the house is curated
through the enfilade to the eastern edge.

Craignish
In topography

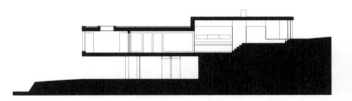

Craignish
Section

Externally we also wish to create comfortable and sheltered microclimates in our northern latitude, by designing with the landscape to create courtyards and sheltered gardens, such as at Lunga again, while also controlling and orchestrating the impact of existing views from within, as at Craignish, where a framed view from the kitchen also acts as a window seat.

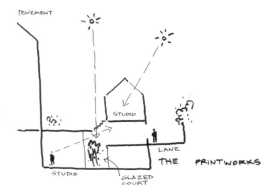

Printworks: sketch section with light well sunk into the heart of the plan.

← Craignish
  "The Enfilade" with window seat.

↓ Printworks: spatial relationships
  over two levels.

Tarvie Lodge bathroom "periscope" sectional study model, exploring the use of passive ventilation, while capturing views to the hills through the periscopic arrangement of window and mirror.

Tarvie Lodge in the landscape.

Tarvie Lodge elevation/section

The tools that we as architects use to develop the design are the drawings of plans and sections, diagrammatic at the start and using precedents that we know or find out about that relate to the problem or to our initial ideas. As Peter Zumthor has said, "Practicing architecture is asking oneself questions".[3]

We may draw the site in a number of different ways, trying to fully understand it, and imagine how people will move around the design, considering arrival sequences and practical and aesthetic controls of views and movement, with lobbies and dégagements, as in the entrance to the coastal house at Cove. We will also employ Beaux Arts devices such as enfilades, which in the house at Craignish link all the main rooms at the upper level to a long gallery that enjoys the best views. Quick models are also useful to help imagine spaces, and to clarify how light may be best introduced into them, which we have done in a rather dramatic way for the bathrooms at Tarvie, giving them light and a view that they would not perhaps be expected to have.

We will also employ a range of devices that link the spaces and manipulate the section, which is the key to the design of our office building at the Printworks. Employing an intuitive shorthand of scribbles and thoughts understood specifically by us all allows very quick reactions and helps spark further ideas. We may invert the normal in a playful manner, by, for example, trying to make an opening rather than to "insert an object", and trial different typologies that are well understood to us in different contexts. This is an intense and iterative process. Some designs may come more easily and even appear to have an inevitability about them, others may only emerge after many different attempts and are the result of considerable struggle.

To quote Alvar Aalto again, "It is not what a building looks like on the day that it is opened but what it is like thirty years later that matters".[4]

All of our projects have been tailored to meet the needs of particular clients who may eventually move on, and we hope that the buildings will serve others equally well: architectural ideas are bigger and last longer than individual whims.

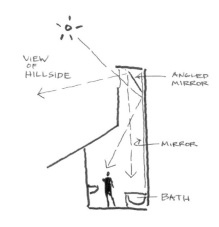

Tarvie Lodge bathroom "periscope" section.

1   Alvar Aalto, 'The Trout and the Mountain Stream', 1947. Quoted by Colin St John Wilson in *Architectural Reflections*, Butterworth 1992.
2   Junichiro Tanizaki, *In Praise of Shadows*, Vintage 2001.
3   Peter Zumthor, *Thinking Architecture*, Birkhäuser 1999.
4   Quoted by Colin St John Wilson in *The Other Tradition of Modern Architecture*, Academy Editions 1995.

Tarvie Lodge North Gardner Street Printworks

0 1 2   5   10

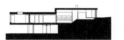  

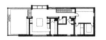  

Craignish   House at Lunga   Cove

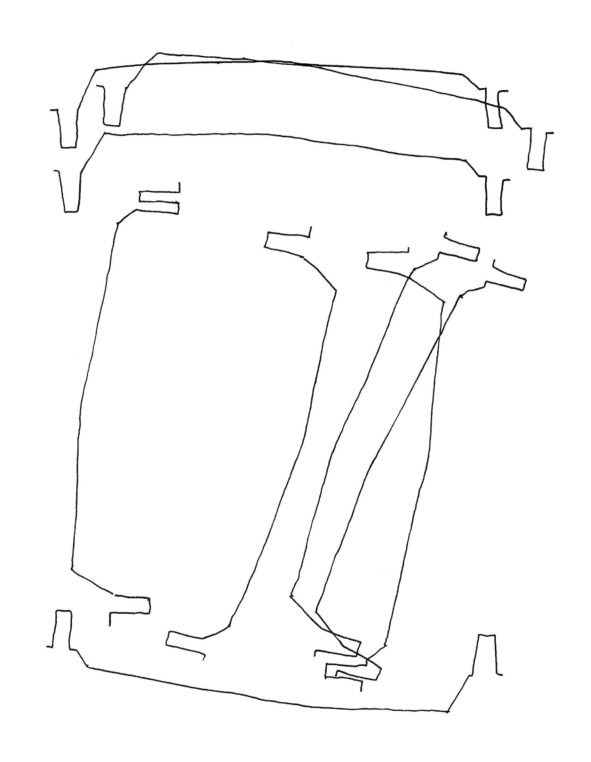

4 — ANATOMY OF A TERRACE OR A DWELLING IN FOUR PARTS BY TWO AUTHORS

Henry McKeown & Ian Alexander jmarchitects

A *terraced* or *terrace house* (UK) or *townhouse* (US) is a term in architecture and city planning referring to a style of medium-density housing that originated in Europe in the 16th century, where a row of identical or mirror-image houses share side walls (sometimes known as 'party' walls). They are also known in some areas as row houses or linked houses.

Blackhouses were common to the Highlands of Scotland and Ireland and were long, narrow buildings with 2 rooms, constructed with dry stone walls and a thatched roof. They had no chimneys and consequently soot from the open fire would blacken the thatch, killing bugs and mites. This was replaced every year, and the blackened thatch was reused as fertiliser.

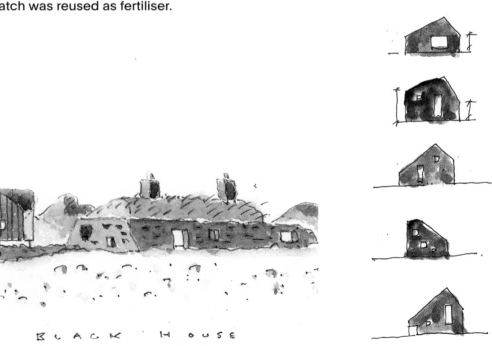

BLACK HOUSE

Gable studies

Blackhouse, reimagined

Blackhouse

TERRACE PROFILES.

Terrace

By its very nature the terrace mode of dwelling is a collective model. It is a shared mode which requires privacy, individuality and ownership. Terrace architecture often achieves its virtues and character through a rigorous use of repetitive elements with only subtle inflexions that define important parts of the dwelling, for example a gable end (the end of the row) or important corners.

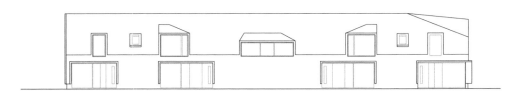

Street elevation

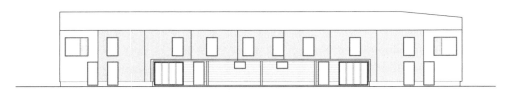

Garden elevation

The Inverness Terrace (Stealth House) was an opportunity for us to reconsider the concept of contextual regionalism; the idea of appropriateness and a sense of belonging in architecture. The idea of the terrace typology appealed to us and gave us a chance to reconsider and reinterpret the traditional terrace format in a fresh way. Our analyses and reflections on the blackhouse and the vernacular led us to a dissection of the terrace model into its key architectural components, which in turn led to a recomposition of the part, namely the roof, the gable, the window, the dormer and the plan configuration. It also led to the reinterpretation of the building form, its scale and its materiality, which we used to help model a new version of this familiar housing typology.

Gable studies

Manipulating the section

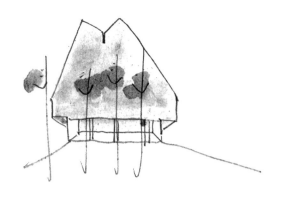

A deep interest in simple forms stems also from our early research and reading of the Italian neo-rationalists, particularly Aldo Rossi and Giorgio Grassi, and the fascination of these two in a reductive architecture. In other words, architectural form that is distilled from the historic context of a region, is characterised by a sparseness of detail and ornament and is informed by the local vernacular. In the case of Rossi and Grassi, an innate subconscious sense of 'Italianisms' pervades.

This interest manifested itself in a parallel obsession with European vernacular architecture – in particular agrarian architecture. Often observed and drawn by us while travelling, this is an architecture of necessity which could be described as 'un-designed' in the professional sense and is born out of a direct, formal response to function, locality, climate and context.

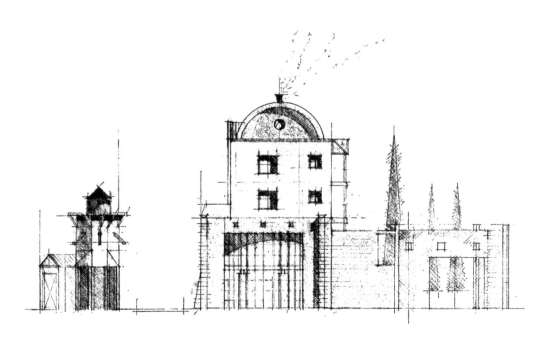

Student thesis sketch, Mackintosh School of Architecture, 1985.

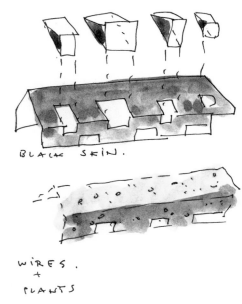

BLACK HOUSE.

BLACK SKIN.

WIRES.
+
PLANTS

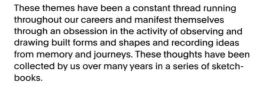

Drawing the idea: a graphical brief

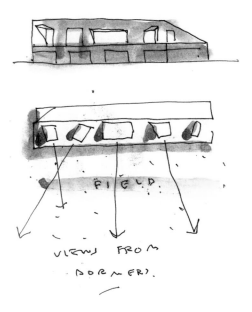

LOW PROFILE.
'STEALTH LIKE'

FIELD.

VIEWS FROM
DORMERS.

These themes have been a constant thread running throughout our careers and manifest themselves through an obsession in the activity of observing and drawing built forms and shapes and recording ideas from memory and journeys. These thoughts have been collected by us over many years in a series of sketchbooks.

More recently, a number of these ideas have directly informed our work, both built and unbuilt. It is interesting to reflect on this unselfconscious activity of repeatedly observing and drawing such formal elements: gables, profiles, chimneys, dormers, snoods and projections.

Blackhouse, reimagined (façade detail)

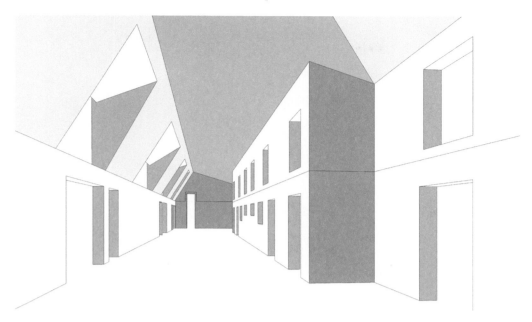

Shell study (inside the section)

The Stealth House was conceived in a collaborative discourse between both authors. By reflecting on this project together for this book, we realised that there was a subconscious appreciation and a shared admiration for the *un-designed* and how the *un-designed* might inspire the *designed*.

In this illustrated essay we also use drawing as a means to capture how our thoughts have evolved and developed in the past and could potentially be developed in our future work. The purpose of our enquiry is to fundamentally think about the nature of dwelling within the context of the terrace house typology.

It is easy to understand how two architects who have worked side by side for almost 30 years can share a similar fascination and obsession with a particular way of making architecture. We have a constant need to record rudimentary building forms in our notebooks, each sketch distinct and individual in character and in the drawing technique and medium.

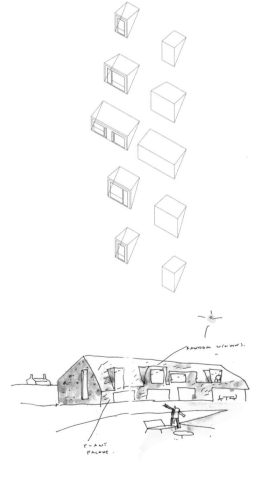

Apertures and views:
↑ James Turrell, *Knight Rise*, 2001
→ Silhouette, dormer and external skin detail

On reflection, it is apparent that this shared architectural empathy sits at the core of our architectural value system and this fascination can be traced back to our student days and to the architects we studied and read at architecture school. It is also evident in the body of work we have amassed over our careers. This is informed by what we have subconsciously absorbed, and how, in our own individual way, this underlying formal architectural language has established itself in our work. As our work has matured, we have made our own interpretations of this architectural phenomenon. This is why the Stealth House project, of all our projects we have designed together, illustrates this collaborative journey most revealingly.

In our understanding, Rossi's reference to architectural autonomy, namely going beyond mere function, is important to us. It suggests an architecture with a self-referential quality that creates a familiar relationship with the context of both landscape and city but is also deeply rooted in history and collective memory. As noted in Peter Buchanan's essay, writing on the subject of the Italian neo-rationalists: 'Rossi instead distils history into forms that still look modern in their abstraction yet are fairly traditional in composition.'[1]

← Blackhouse, reimagined

1   Peter Buchanan, 'Aldo Rossi: silent monuments', *Architectural Review*, Vol. CLXXII, No. 1028, October 1982, pp.48–54.

The anatomy of the terrace is a touch-stone for some of this shared thinking and although the focus is on the terrace and its architectural intentions, ideas, associations and interests, we illustrate how we also deliberately experiment with drawings as a way of 'seeing' possibilities of space, volume and form in an abstract way, rather than in the sense of a fully designed building interior. In order to make explicit our approach to design, we have created a series of drawings and reference images that try to illustrate a design narrative for this simple building.

How do we make these investigations? Firstly by selecting a series of images that represent these innate values and are fundamental to our thinking, for example the blackhouse, the window,

the oculus. By rotating, dissecting and observing, we offer the drawings as a meditation on the proposal. The purpose of the drawing is something we foster within the practice in parallel with the recording of ideas in order that the work is durable enough to withstand critical scrutiny. An interest in art practice and its architectural referencing and the phenomenological aspects of sky, landscape and city is also important to us.

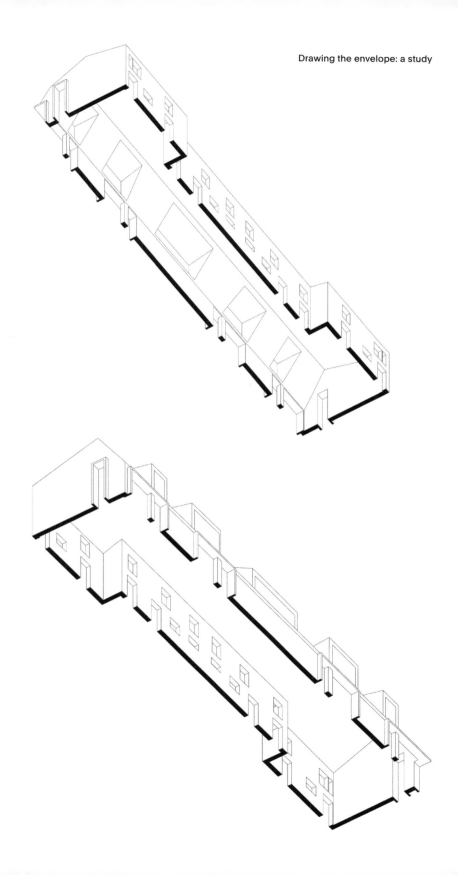

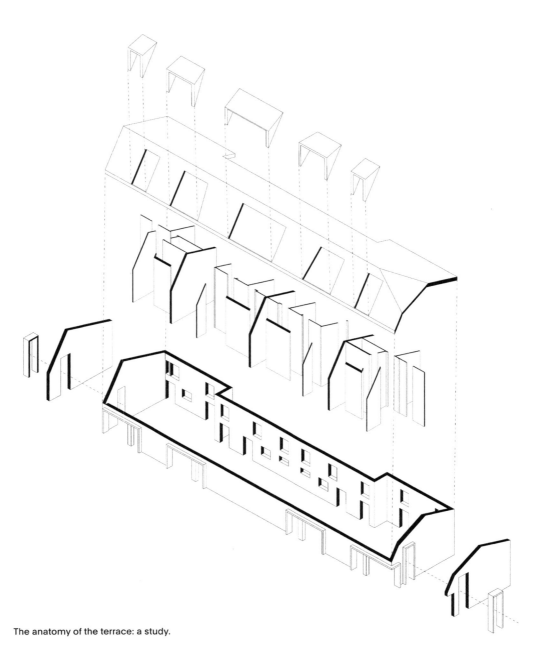

The anatomy of the terrace: a study.

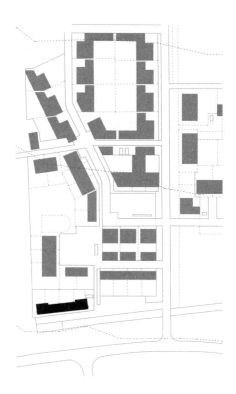

Locality plan

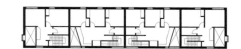

Elevation

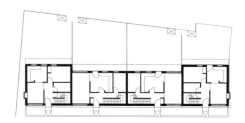

First floor plan

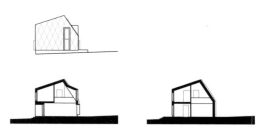

Ground floor plan

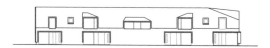

Gable: elevation/sections

81

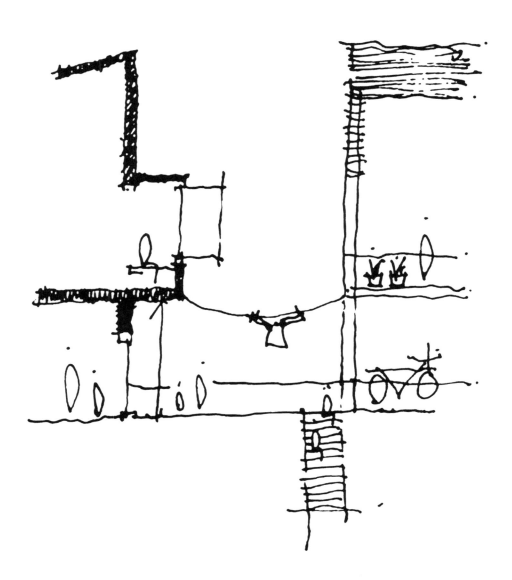

5 — NEIGHBOURLINESS

Stacey Phillips
Gordon Murray
Architects

It is our belief that social housing projects invariably contribute to sustainable design, not solely through the use of materials or technologies but also through the underpinning of existing communities. This ambition reinforces ideals of how fundamental high-quality design is to everyday lives and raises a key question about whether small-scale architectural moves can encourage interaction and inclusion within communities and result in a greater degree of neighbourliness.

Telford Drive – crafted detail

Telford Drive is a housing development for Manor Estates Housing Association in Edinburgh completed in 2006. The project brings together a landlocked 'wasteland' site and an established local authority estate with the key objective of reinforcing a strong sense of community and identity for both new and existing residents. This challenge demanded exploration of fundamental principles. Themes such as threshold, interaction, individualism, privacy, openness, belonging, ownership and pride are all critical concepts within this project which position the needs of the residents as the principal focus within the design criteria.

The design of Telford Drive developed with a belief that designing buildings as positive additions to the built environment could act as a mechanism for positive cultural change. The place, the local community and local culture provided a vital springboard from which architecture could emerge. Getting close to the life of the residents was the starting point.

What defines community in this context? A group, individuals, families, the elderly, the young – people with unfamiliar lives entwined purely by the shared place in which they live? Architectural attitudes or elements therefore become significant as potential devices for providing opportunities to unify people by virtue of them sharing a place.

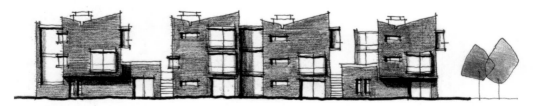

Initial concept sketch exploring ideas of softness.

Architects are trained to challenge conventions rather than simply repeat solutions – questioning what the first principles might be in a design problem. Interrogating potentially ill-considered assumptions about people's lives and behaviours is vital. Understanding the nature of the place is fundamental to the successful integration of new buildings. How the character of place is represented and how the fabric has developed over time all inform design decisions. Every social housing project is unique and contains specific challenges. The key question in this instance resulted from a desire for the architecture to encourage or reinforce a sense of belonging to the place. We envisaged a serene, dignified expression generating a calm background for life to exist and human spirits to be lifted.

As architects we are attracted by the fruitful occupation of space by people. At Telford Drive, the simple expression of life as revealed on the inhabited balconies of the surrounding 1950s local authority blocks, from washing lines to budgie cages, gardens to workshops, provided a spatial, social and cultural reference which we thought could immediately connect old and new. We were encouraged by how this anonymous architecture could accommodate and support everyday life in such a relaxed manner.

Supporting this notion, a series of simple architectural devices were explored by us with the intention of choreographing elements to quietly influence different ways of living. These we hoped would provide opportunities to inhabit a place which suited both the individual and the collective, allowing residents to be individual as well as communal.

Juhani Pallasmaa, in his book *The Eyes of the Skin*, explains how:

> The timeless task of architecture is to create embodied and lived existential metaphors that concretise and structure our being in the world. Architecture reflects, materialises and eternalises ideas and images of ideal life. Buildings … enable us to structure, understand and remember the shapeless flow of reality and, ultimately, to recognise and remember who we are …

First floor plan/terrace level

Ground floor plan

Levels of raised ground move out from the centre of the site, essentially a shared, intimate landscaped space which is open to all residents. Secondary spaces filter through subtle steps in the ground plane, from entirely public through semi-private to private gardens at the buildings' edges. Adoption of these spaces is encouraged and ownership established by a graduation of defined thresholds. A 'carved' terraced block made up of four brick 'towers', which at first floor cantilever off a podium, forms the twenty homes establishing the overall project. A series of steps fold up from the ground to connect to a series of elevated terraces between the towers.

This space, shared physically between two homes only, mirrors the balconies of its neighbours. The terrace on one level detaches the residents from the street life below, becoming a private area for play with washing lines or a threshold between inside and outside living. Equal opportunity exists for the terrace to become an invited space for social gatherings, which is encouraged by visual connections to the street and windows above. The simple articulation of these spaces is through the materials of warm brick and timber. A sense of protection and enclosure embody similar ambitions to those seen in the work of Alvar Aalto, whose interest often lay in the encounter with a space or an object as a sensory human experience, rather than an exercise in formal aesthetics.

The space informs how the human body feels within it through its proportions, quality of light, and the reverberations and the softness of sound. The scale of the terraces is appropriate, embracing the residents and creating a cosy sense of 'room' at the heart of the home; a symbolic campfire for the community.

Existing neighbours: 1950s local authority housing allowing personalisation and expression of life through individual balconies.

Bay windows open out to form balconies allowing for both personalisation and interaction.

Breaking down the scale of the proposals through the articulation of the massing reinforces the ideas of social interaction while ensuring appropriate degrees of privacy are achieved. The shared terraces and central 'village green' are complemented by a series of conservatories, winter gardens and balconies giving multiple properties a connection to the spaces and the neighbouring buildings. The design itself promotes choice. Residents are provided with private space which they can adapt, and many opportunities exist to engage with neighbours. By forming deep projections of the façade, the winter gardens' depth prevents any view extending into the home while also doubling as a balcony space. Parents can watch their children playing below or talk to a neighbour by opening the façade. Vertical staggering of the winter gardens results in an informality and individuality in the buildings' architectural expression.

Careful consideration was given to the selection of materials and architectural detailing. Ensuring a reserved and restrained modesty for the buildings was a conscious design approach, reflecting a resourcefulness in the face of tight budgetary constraints. The slight contrast in the palette of bricks, the cantilever of the first floor and the soft pitching of the roof line all break with the conventions of low-rise housing blocks. We hope that a sense of warmth and compassion finds expression within the buildings. The 'softness' of complementary brick and larch provides a sense of quality and a respect for the craft of making and building. As a result, a familiarity of elements and materials provide a sense of place and shared belonging underpinning the aspirations we hope of those who live there.

Our desire as architects is to embed character and qualities in a space which enable the occupant to fruitfully inhabit and feel a tangible sense of dwelling and as a consequence, belonging. The objects which turn a house into a home cannot be defined by architecture but can nevertheless be supported by it. This is what we believe the culture of architecture is – placing people first through dignified and appropriate design. Telford Drive is a happy place to live.

A house is a home when it shelters the body and comforts the soul…

Phillip Moffat

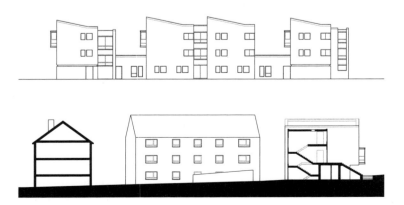

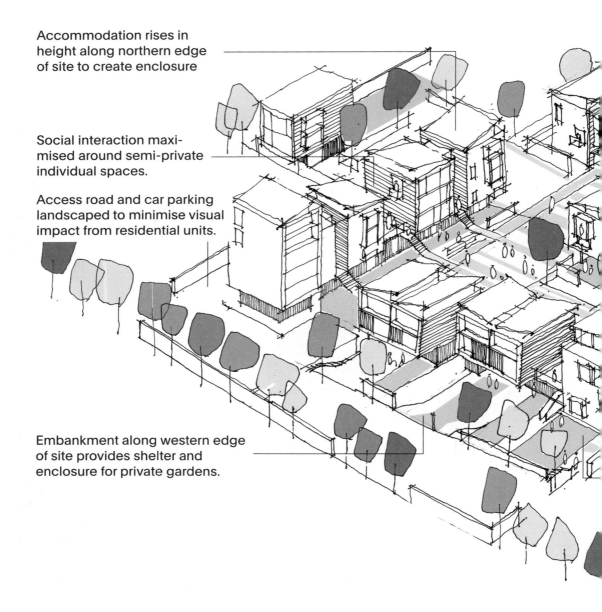

Accommodation rises in height along northern edge of site to create enclosure

Social interaction maximised around semi-private individual spaces.

Access road and car parking landscaped to minimise visual impact from residential units.

Embankment along western edge of site provides shelter and enclosure for private gardens.

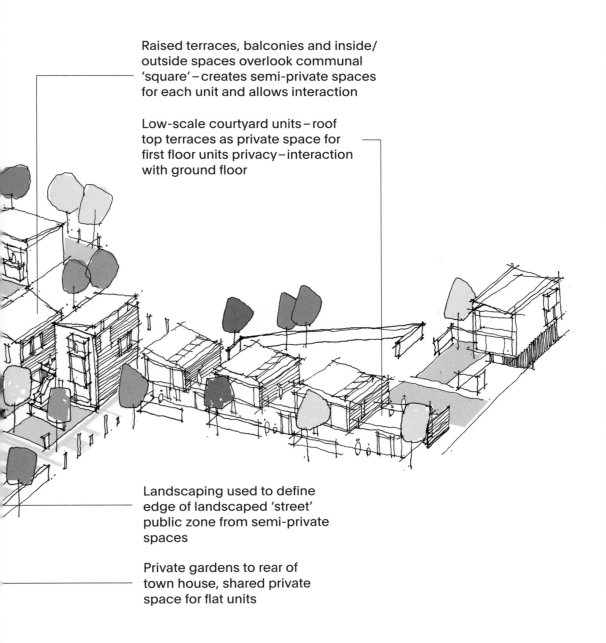

Raised terraces, balconies and inside/
outside spaces overlook communal
'square' – creates semi-private spaces
for each unit and allows interaction

Low-scale courtyard units – roof
top terraces as private space for
first floor units privacy – interaction
with ground floor

Landscaping used to define
edge of landscaped 'street'
public zone from semi-private
spaces

Private gardens to rear of
town house, shared private
space for flat units

Site location plan

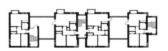

Section/elevations

Section/elevations

First floor plan and elevation

Ground floor plan and elevation

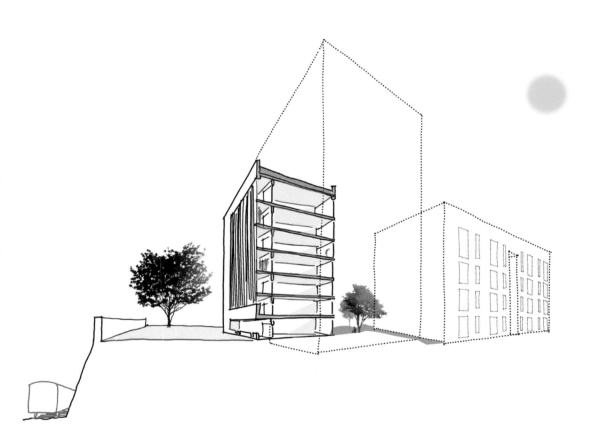

6 — CAUSALITY AND THE GENESIS OF TYPOLOGY

Adrian Stewart
DO Architecture

We believe there is an intrinsic connection between the physical layout of a space and the psychological and behavioural impact of this space upon its user, and we think that this is particularly significant in the design of housing. With this in mind, we have a particular interest in nuancing the format and detail of such spaces, and in particular the edge conditions that delineate territories and thresholds between public, semi-private and private spaces.

In our design process, we try to embrace the phenomenon of causality[1] (cause and effect) in how we learn from the past to help inform our current and indeed future decisions. An acknowledgement of this helps to equip us through acquired knowledge of recent as well as historic precedents. In our view, this sits comfortably alongside the demands of working with an urban Registered Social Landlord (RSL) whose projects are generally density-sensitive and demand a careful balance between a sense of place and community and an economy of scale.

The increased density required when building on a small footprint or with poor ground conditions often necessitates that the building must be taller than in other, more conventional situations. The task of the architect in this scenario is often to facilitate the desired density without losing the socially cohesive qualities more often associated with lower density housing. Using these principles, we have focused on one particular typology in the Govanhill area of South Glasgow, creating 46 new urban flatted dwellings in a seven-storey development for a large RSL. Achieving this balance required a

thorough investigative analysis ranging from urban strategy to the minutiae of physical detail in order to explore, understand, test and respond to some very specific characteristics of the site, our client and current regulations. The outcome of this process steered the building typology and form towards the model of a medium-rise open access deck solution, which in the UK at least has often had negative associations.

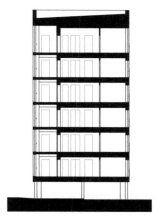

↑ Cross section through
main Pavilion Block
← Pavilion Block cutaway

1   *Causality* (also referred to as *causation,* or cause and effect) is the agency or efficacy that connects one process (the cause) with another process or state (the effect), where the first is understood to be partly responsible for the second, and the second is dependent on the first. In general, an effect has many causes, which are said to be causal factors for it, and all lie in its past. An effect can in turn be a cause of many other effects.

As our design developed, we established some clear parameters which attempted to both create the required density and encourage a sense of community and neighbourliness. This may sound like a generic, all-embracing strap line, but we mean it at a simple level, namely to create places which people can consider their home; places they can identify with and make their own. This aspiration, however, is achieved more often in low-rise terraced and tenemental properties than in open access deck housing. In order to reconsider the open access deck typology as a potential solution, we established a set of clear parameters within which we worked as follows:

PLACEMAKING AT THE HEART OF AN URBAN RESPONSE

Our particular approach to delivering affordable housing at this location on the edge of Glasgow city centre informed the planning and massing decisions to reconcile density with human scale. Our urban response to the urban park characteristics of our site places a seven-storey block at the site's north boundary alongside a four-storey companion block at the west boundary. These defined a strong edge condition and completed the framing and sense of enclosure of the park. These also featured open access balconies providing both (what we hoped would be) animated glimpses of life in the building and dramatic views outwards over the city towards the distant landscape beyond.

INSTILLING A SENSE OF OWNERSHIP THROUGH TENURE AND DEMOCRACY

This was achieved through consciously designing places which would encourage residents to personalise them and as a result, to create an identity that directly speaks to them. In order to facilitate this ambition, we created an exterior 'defensible' zone on the open access deck that permitted the residents to have some agency over the space immediately outside their flat. The precise format, materiality and scale of this semi-private space became pivotal in testing options for this development. A larger access deck width than the norm was established to accomodate what in essence is a 'privacy strip' to the main public circulation space. The precise calibration of this was important to avoid them becoming so wide as to compromise daylight penetration into the flats.

→ Top: Caledonian Mansions, Kelvinbridge, Glasgow (James Miller 1897). A Victorian-era precedent of the open access deck typology which remains popular and effective in addressing densified elevated circulation.

→ Bottom: Pavilion and Companion blocks viewed from Larkfield Street. The taller pavilion block addresses the city scale to the north, while the companion block steps down to address the tenemental scale of Govanhill.

Well-known examples such as Park Hill in Sheffield, where the 'street in the sky' concept established a series of access decks that were designed to facilitate the traffic of milk floats to drive along them, have been less successful socially. Such arrangements did not permit adequate daylight or sunlight to reach the outer walls of the homes or encourage personalisation of spaces outside each home. As a result, these open decks were not used in a social or neighbourly way as intended but in fact became spaces which quickly took on anti-social characteristics. It was our ambition to provide each dwelling with its own external access to the outside world, much like a traditional house or cottage flat would have, whether it be at ground level or seven storeys higher.

ENABLING IMMEDIATE TERRITORY WITHIN PUBLIC SPACE TO BELONG TO THE HOME

The opportunities presented by open access decks beyond the improved density allowed external windows on both sides of the property, which in turn had advantages of enhanced sunlight, daylight and cross-ventilation. Windows at both ends of the property and at the open access deck side in particular established a strong visual connection between inside and out. As a result, the main entry door is no longer the only interface with the access deck but is also a window to a habitable room. This also established a new connection and source of informal supervision from inside to outside and as a consequence, the distance created between the access deck and each dwelling by the privacy strip discourages passers-by from peering into the flat.

SENSE OF SECURITY (SPACE TO SIT/SPACE TO PASS/ SPACE TO PAUSE)

The privacy strip described above is given a slightly different treatment to delineate it from the general circulation space alongside it. This treatment not only visually distinguishes it from the general circulation space but also provides a place which can be inhabited by the person living within, hopefully encouraging the arrival of plants and informal seating in warmer seasons.

Personal space

Social space

Comfortable space

Analysis of personal space

Elevation

Section

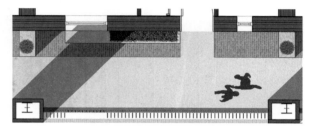

Plan

Open access circulation occupation and edge condition studies.

→ Left page: Private Courtyard viewed from the
  Companion Block. The internal corner held between
  the Pavilion and Companion blocks creates a private
  garden space, overlooked by and supervised from the
  occupied access deck.

→ Right page: Companion Block viewed from Private
  Internal Courtyard. The fully permeable screen and
  deep occupied deck behind establish a strong visual
  connection between Companion Block and Private
  Courtyard.

ENCOURAGING LINGERING AND DISCOURAGING SCURRYING

Our very detailed study into an appropriate deck proportion, size and overall design, hopefully encourages residents to stop and chat with each other. We think that encouraging neighbourliness is facilitated by creating quality spaces where people naturally pass each other and where they may be inclined to stop and chat. Such spaces might also include a vista over the city, but crucially they are spaces where residents do not perceive themselves to be blocking the circulation route. We have found that these accidental meeting spaces can reduce inhibitions for casual chatting between neighbours. This may occur on the enhanced access deck or on the stair landings – all of which as a result may help instil a sense of belonging and community within the development.

VISIBILITY AND CONNECTION TO AND THROUGH THE SPACE (PROPORTION, OPENNESS AND VIEWS TO NEIGHBOURS)

We feel that the sense of enclosure of the open access decks is absolutely critical to their success as social as well as functional architectural elements. Some post-war municipal examples deploy very narrow decks with solid balustrades which can sometimes feel impersonal and precarious. In order to encourage social inhabitation of the open access decks, we designed full height vertical fin elements spanning from floor to ceiling. These provide a particular kind of enclosure, while also permitting extensive views across the city and generous daylight, as well as creating supervised spaces which are comfortable to walk, stop, talk or even play within.

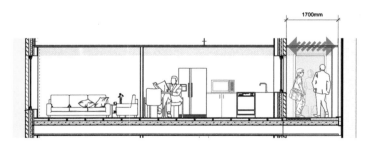

1700mm

Traditional 'narrow' open access deck.

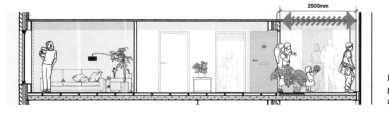

2500mm

Enhanced width deck providing 'defensible space' adjacent to apartment.

Access Deck Proportion Study: testing the effectiveness of enhanced deck proportions to create defensible space and sense of ownership within a semi-private circulation route.

Companion Block Access Deck: an enhanced deck width and permeable edge strengthens a visual connection with the courtyard and encourages occupation and 'ownership' of this space.

ESTABLISHMENT OF AN APPROPRIATE LANDING LENGTH

We established that five flats per landing was appropriate to create a compact space that had social potential while not appearing merely as an external 'corridor' to circulate through. Density is critical in new urban developments, and the open access deck can be a very useful device to unlock shared spaces which can, as a result, enhance a sense of community. When density is pushed too far, the danger of consequential anonymity is high. This can impact negatively on any ambitions to create a neighbourly environment and result in long-term problems and difficult living conditions for the residents, which has been the case historically in Park Hill or in Belfast's Divis Flats.

In the development of ideas for this project and through researching the history of the deck access typology, we have been influenced greatly in our design process, at both an urban and a detail scale, by the phenomenon of cause and effect. Through our design process, we think we have established an appropriate, contemporary housing typology design. Through a renewed and informed analysis of the deck access typology we think our design solution will encourage neighbourliness and community activity and not be associated with the negative connotations of the past.

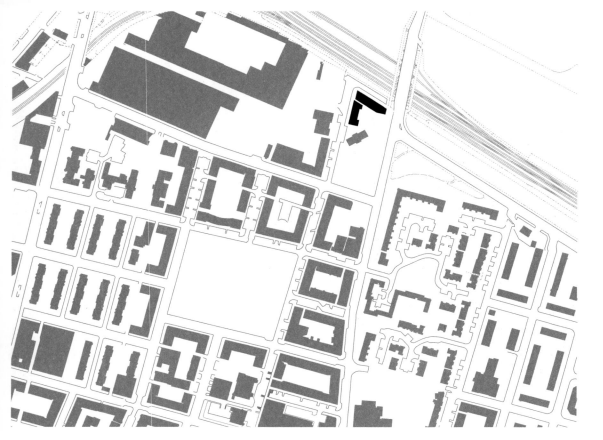

Site location plan

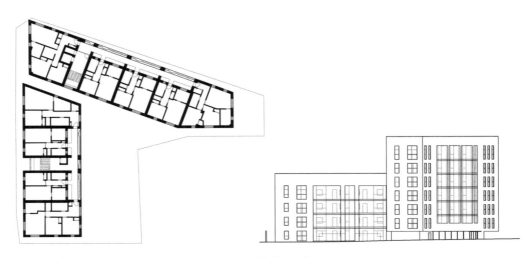

Upper level plan

East elevation

Pavilion section

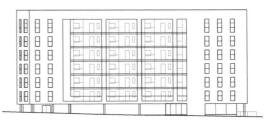

Pavilion block north elevation

7 — THE PALAZZO, THE KEEP AND THE COMPENDIUM OF A CITY

Stephen Hoey
Elder & Cannon
Architects

Elegant piers and lintels in trabeatum form the colonnade of the rooftop loggia of The Palazzo of the Jesuit Priests of St Aloysius' College on top of the highest drumlin in the centre of the City of Glasgow.

The loggia is a room; one of many in the compendium of the Palazzo, which contains reception, prayer, dining, study, library, bed and living rooms. Neither inside nor completely outside, the loggia is a threshold expanded to form a space particular to an ancient dwelling typology, namely the urban townhouse. It is a private amenity space; at one level practically function-al. It is a useful external area which allows a set-back living room to enjoy a full expanse of south facing glass, yet be screened from a range of classroom windows on the opposite side of the street. It also serves another ancient purpose. As a space of contemplation, relaxation and repose in the heart of the city, it offers the necessary experi-ence of phenomena. In this room, breeze brushes the skin, light dances on the eyes, rain falls in meditative liquid sounds, tastes and fragrances grow, linger and fade. Direct contact with climate makes it a place of the body, mind and senses.

It is a crafted space made from sand-stone quarried and riven to form a floor; sawn and dressed timber frames with large sliding screens of glass. Bricks of white china clay cut from a black German forest form two walls. The fine concrete colonnade is a mix of cement, coastal aggregate and fine white Port-land sand cast in steel until set, washed and honed to a hard polished finish. The partially covered roof is mined mineral zinc.

'Architecture is the art of reconciliation between ourselves and the world, and this mediation takes place through the senses' J. Pallasmaa

The majority of the room is open to the sky and such exposure will bring patina and shade to the materials which to the touch are smooth, course, textured and fine. It will mature through nature and climate, and it will measure time through light and shade. This man-made, yet natural space hosts flora and fauna. In this room, spring wakes in yellow, pink and violet. Summer is verdent, lush, long and glistening, winter fruits in purple, browns and deep blues, and autumn burns amber, red and ochre. The seasons bring layers of texture, reflecting colours through light and liquid, and these phenomena define particular qualities and the changing character of the loggia.

This room is a barometer, a bellwether, recording the grain and texture of our experience of the city, climate and phenomena. It is a calm and silent witness to time. From outside below, the fine delicate tracery of the colonnade is silhouetted on the changing shadow of the loggia. Depth and weight bring presence to a detail within the compendium of the street. These details narrate the archaeology, morphology and rich, varied typology of the campus and the neighbourhood.

Spires define chapels, domes and cupolas churches, heavy sculpted porches and balconies villas, gables and reflective expanses of glass define school buildings, and the hand scale of bricks suggests domesticity and dwelling. These are punctuations in the symphony of the street, which is textured by rhythms of topography and the repetitive pattern of tenemental and Victorian classroom windows.

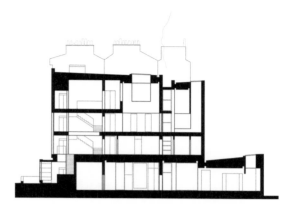

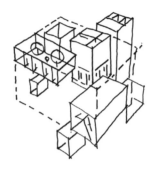

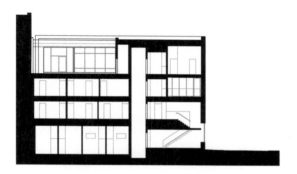

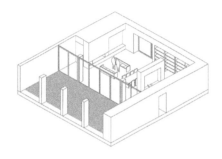

The Compendium of the Rooms in
The Compendium of the City.

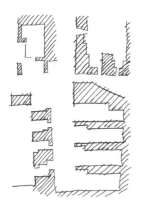

On the plateau of Laurieston, only fragments and ruins of an old order remain. Void and the tabula rasa dominate. The compendium is formed from memory. Context is formed by historic images of tenements lining streets like strong mute regimental guards solemn and civic in stature.

Now a new tenement stands similarly austere, heavy and sculptural with considered proportion and stature. Alone it guards the landscape like an historic keep. Stoic. *The keep of Gorbals, Laurieston and Cumberland.*

It is silent and solid. Hundreds of thousands of bricks have been laid by hand in repetitive geometric folding patterns creating depth within the envelope, space within the elevation. Ingoes, porches, doorways are the thresholds celebrating the moment inside becomes outside.

Fashioned through a process of firing twice in a kiln and levelled by the craftsman, air drawn at a precise moment, the brick is heavily textured and varied in colour. It is grey, green, blue, purple and changes in hue and tone with the time of day and month. It is tactile, hard, strong and coarse. Cedar lines a part of the outdoor room. Scented, it is soft to the touch. Absorbent, it offers a particular acoustic quality to this almost private, special place. As afternoon draws, western light falls on fine bronze metalwork. Delicate shadows cast on silhouettes framed by the large window reflecting the golden evening sun.

Elevation

Elevation

Cross section through courtyard

Typical upper floor plan

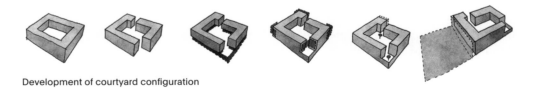

Development of courtyard configuration

The west wall is deep. An array of horizontal and vertical terraces creates an inhabited façade which is host to the personal accoutrements of the dwellings' inhabitants. Ornamental china and clay pottery, plants, elegant suspended mobiles rotate in the breeze, chairs, tables, clothes drying, toys, cups, glasses and bottles and books – the paraphernalia of life. Sometimes a carefully controlled arrangement and presentation of private personalities is revealed in public. On the terrace a mother and child sit quietly in the fresh air; couples old and young discuss their day around tables of food where generations of families gather and children play patterning the sound of the place. Everyday life is received by the architecture.

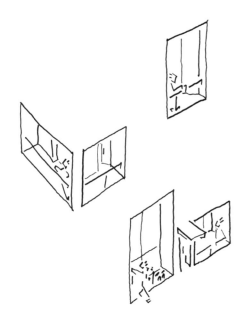

These open living rooms offer another layer to the grain of the compendium of the city. They present an engaging narrative insight into the lives of the dwellings in a very particular place which is both private and public. They are places of protected family intimacy on the threshold of the civic realm, where they become a series of individual yet shared social events.

They are valuable life-enhancing extensions of the privacy of the homes, offering both practical functional space and the opportunity to engage with nature, phenomena and climate in a secure place which encourages repose. They promote expression and communication and texture the environment, defining character and our sense of place. Through craft they bring depth, sculptural weight and substance, and offer the imaginative, poetic interpretations of identity. The narratives of the places we call home, where a house becomes a *Palazzo,* a tenement is a Keep and a collection of memories of details is *The Compendium of a City.*

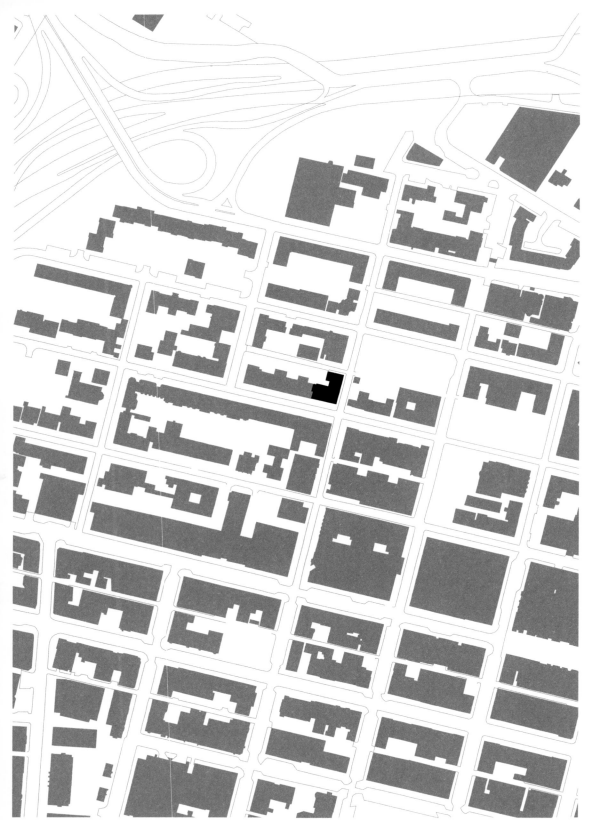

Site location plan

Front elevation

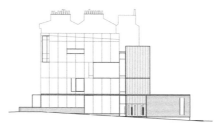

Side elevation

Long section

Cross section

Plan at loggia level

Site location plan

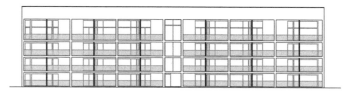

Elevation

Cross section through courtyard

Typical upper floor plan

Elevation

ESSAYS

INNOVATION AND
TRADITION
Dick van Gameren

'THE BLINDED MAN
SEES WITH HIS EARS
AND HANDS'
MODES OF DWELLING
Simon Henley

DWELLING – ON LESSONS
AND PRACTICES IN
ARCHITECTURE
Graeme Hutton

INNOVATION
AND TRADITION

Dick van Gameren

The idea that the development of twentieth-century modern architecture constitutes a linear and inevitable step in the evolution of the art of building has long since made way for a much more nuanced and layered perspective. The relationship between past and present is a complex one. Innovation can spring from a return to past practices, while clinging to an obsessive idea of the new can just as easily lead to stagnation. Looking back on the architecture of housing over the past 150 years, we can see a recurring orientation on forms from the past, albeit one that's informed by changing motivations and with different outcomes.

In recent years residential architecture has been awash with developments in which abstraction or imitation of familiar, traditional forms appears to be the new lingua franca in housing, spoken by designers with the reputation of innovator or traditionalist. However, the plethora of motives that, in the past century, have informed the renewed orientation on tradition appears to have been sharply reduced: from outspoken views on social reform and improvement of living conditions then, to just trying to keep up with social and political 'trends' today. The use of traditional forms is no longer a means with which to direct the ongoing process of innovation, but an end in itself. The Dutch writer P. F. Thomése put this into words in an essay in the *NRC Handelsblad*: tradition has lost its connotation of passing on methods of working and searching for continuity; it has become a lifestyle. He argues that history, with its embeddedness in time, is losing its meaning.

However, in this interpretation of tradition as a continuity of methods,

improving and adapting over time previously built ideas, lies the fundamental key to housing design. When old forms are merely reproduced and innovation as an inextricable part of tradition is sidelined, then the architecture of housing is also losing its embeddedness and meaning.

This approach to design starting from tradition can literally be rooted in the past, or based on a contemporary starting point, developing this slowly in a tradition of itself.

Examples of the first approach of a strong connection to the past can be found in many works of the British Arts and Crafts architects around 1900. An important source of inspiration for them was the anonymous, traditional and seemingly timeless architecture of 300 years earlier, predating the industrial era. The way the Arts and Crafts architects made use of these sources varies greatly, from imitation, interpretation, abstraction or magnification to even caricaturisation.

The work of Mackay Hugh Baillie Scott (1864–1945) follows the historic examples quite closely, at least in a formal sense. However, aside from these familiar material and formal properties, he displayed in his projects a striking inventiveness in finding new typologies for the mass production of housing. Waterlow Court in Hampstead Garden Suburb in North London is a case in point. The building, one of the very first affordable (at least, at the time of construction) apartment buildings with shared facilities for single occupants, looks like a friendly sixteenth-century university college courtyard building. The architect saw his design as a first step towards an entirely new way of

Well Court in Edinburgh, designed by Sydney Mitchell & Wilson. Tradition and innovation brought together in a remarkable project for collective affordable housing.

living in a suburban setting, where collective housing blocks, for families as well as single people, would provide an alternative to what he thought were dreary suburbs with endless terraced housing. An even more radical example of this approach is his unbuilt design for an apartment building, published in 1906 in his book *Houses and Gardens*. He introduces an ideal plan for an urban apartment, clearly inspired by his designs for small country houses and cottages, in their turn based on traditional centuries-old models for these dwelling figures. The apartments have a typical layout, with inglenooks and a minimum of corridor spaces. The chosen layout with a three-sided orientation makes it necessary to liberate the apartment from the customary perimeter block, instead grouping two apartments around a central staircase as a freestanding small individual building. In his book, Baillie Scott explains his vision of these buildings, placed in a public garden, a park developed along natural lines, with woodlands and streams, thus compensating for the loss of a private domain outside the dwelling. The architect's vision is remarkably similar to the ideas brought forward 20 years later by the pioneering modernists such as Gropius and Le Corbusier.

Examples of the second approach, where architects start a 'new' tradition by carefully developing over time their ideas and designs for housing, can be found in the work of two Dutch architects, Willem van Tijen (1894–1974) and Jacob Bakema (1914–1981). They were both convinced 'modernists' with a strong interest in housing design, Van Tijen a member of CIAM since 1930, Bakema a leading figure of Team Ten in the post-war period.

Van Tijen explored in minute detail the optimal design for a small (*Existenzminimum*) apartment. Following

Gropius' ideal of the high-rise gallery-access apartment building, propagated by him in a series of designs but not yet realised, in 1934 Van Tijen designed and built in Rotterdam the Bergpolder-flat, the first high-rise nine-storey apartment building with gallery access. The design was radical in many aspects; the steel structure, the use of prefab elements, the maximised transparency of both exterior and interior walls, all resulting in an extreme economy of space and material. In following projects, Van Tijen continued to develop this new standard, optimising the layout of the apartments and the quality of construction and detailing. The Zuidpleinflat, the first project Van Tijen could realise after the end of the Second World War in heavily bombed Rotterdam, shows the progress of this development. Minute adjustments in the unit plan are just one aspect of his patient search for the ideal standard. He also invited other architects to collaborate in the design. Gerrit Rietveld designed the big windows of the living rooms. Van Tijen's assistant and colleague at that time, Jacob Bakema, continued this search for an ideal standard in his own projects after he joined Johannes van den Broek in 1948, to form two years later the office of Van den Broek en Bakema, which would became one of the leading post-war Dutch practices, now mostly known for its Brutalist public and institutional buildings. In his housing designs, Bakema addressed the issues of monotony and lack of privacy as two of the disadvantages of the high-rise gallery-access. Building on Van Tijen's work and studies, Bakema introduced the idea of the split-level section with corridors giving access to apartments, combining the efficiency of a gallery-access system with the quality of free orientation in the dwelling units to both sides. In a long series of projects, this idea was developed, tested and improved. One of the first built results can be found in Berlin's

Hansa Viertel, as a striking and sculptural tower block with short internal corridors, ending in collective loggias.

The chosen split-level solutions made it easy to create within a simple continuous structure a strong mix of housing types and unit sizes. The building type thus developed formed an important part of Bakema's housing catalogue, developed over many years and illustrating Bakema's ideal of an 'open society' that allows for the 'individual's right to give personal expression to his philosophy of life'.

However, the pressure in the postwar period for mass production of housing led to the scale of his projects increasing, turning the small scale and size of the Berlin prototype into huge urban 'wall' structures, introducing again problems of anonymity and alienation.

This inspired the next generation of architects to rethink these models again and come up with new solutions.

The architects discussing their work in this publication are showing similar approaches to housing design, starting from a thorough understanding of tradition as a tool, as a method to embed their new architecture in time and context. They demonstrate clearly that housing design is not a stylistic exercise, nor an attempt for continuous invention of things not seen before. Something the projects have in common is that they carefully consider the existing, both as physical structures to connect to and as existing ideas and models for housing design, to reinterpret and further develop.

The carefully illustrated interventions and modifications in Studio KAP's contribution have a validity that goes beyond the individual projects described.

'It requires design insight into what needs to be reconsidered and replaced, and what is best left retained or conserved.' An approach that seems valid to housing design in general; looking for a careful balance between what is known and cared for, and what is new, necessary to answer today's needs.

cameronwebster architects show how a consistent exploration of architectural themes leads to seemingly quite different projects, still all based on the same design methods. In the projects, the search for ways to connect to climate and landscape and make very comfortable inside and outside spaces leads to a gradual development of a vocabulary of linked spaces, movement patterns and manipulated sections. Each project clearly builds on the experience of the previous one.

DO Architecture show in their project for Govanhill in South Glasgow that a critical and analytical reading of past projects, such as the famous Park Hill housing in Sheffield, embraced by Team Ten architects and Jacob Bakema when built, can lead to well-thought-out new interpretations of the 'street in the air'.

The careful reading by Gordon Murray Architects of the context of a new apartment building focuses on the almost-anonymous, modest vocabulary of the neighbouring 1950s local authority housing development in Edinburgh. It results in a surprisingly strong relation between the existing and the new, very expressive and carefully detailed project. The old and new benefit, creating a meaningful connection and a shared sense of place.

'Anatomy of a Terrace', the contribution of jmarchitects, shows how an understanding of the traditional types of the blackhouse and the terraced house lead to a 'typology transfer', thus creating a new and beautiful domestic architecture, not merely based on an abstraction of vernacular, but looking into possibilities of space, light and connection to the surrounding landscape and cityscape.

Elder & Cannon refer to their projects as the Palazzo and the Keep, again an obvious reference to traditional typologies, both local and international, as starting points for their design. They are not direct visual imitations, but reinterpretations of the specific spatial and material qualities of these types, leading to projects firmly anchored in their sites. It is striking how, within the restrictions of contemporary housing design, the idea of the solid wall being at the same time a space in between, so fantastically explored in the austere, introverted medieval Scottish keeps, is reinvented in the Laurieston project.

An exceptional project is Orkidstudio's Hellen's House, designed and built in a very different context, that of rural Kenya. An inventive use of locally produced and available building materials results in an affordable and beautiful private house. The built project will hopefully become an example for others building their homes, showing a very affordable way to achieve a much higher quality of construction than is common practice at this moment. The introduction of this new type, which looks like it has always been there, rooted in context and everyday life, will hopefully start a new tradition, a new vernacular.

In all examples, the orientation on an architecture shaped by local customs and traditions, comes to the fore as a means to innovation. In this connection of tradition and innovation lies the power of the architecture of housing; it acknowledges the need for domestic spaces that can be recognised as such and be appropriated, spaces rooted in time, answering the desire for a private, constant place in a surrounding world that seems to change faster and faster; the desire for a sense of place.

A GENEALOGY OF COLLECTIVE LIVING IN BRITAIN

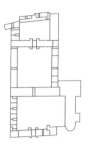

Haddon Hall Derbyshire	St. John's College Cambridge	Hardwick Hall Derbyshire	Ragely Hall Warwickshire	The Albany London	Well Hall Edinburgh

Courtyard

Central Hall

1400	1500	1600	1680	1770	1890

Haddon Hall great hall	St. John's College great hall	Hardwick Hall long gallery	Ragely Hall great hall	The Albany outdoor gallery	Well Hall club room and apartments facing the terrace

Vitruvius Britannicus,
Colin Campbell,
1715–1725

A genealogy of collective living in Britain,
compiled by Dick van Gameren for the RIBA exhibition
At Home in Britain, 2016.

Albert Court London	Waterlow Court London	Highpoint II London	Keeling House London	Cripps Building St. Johns College Cambridge	Mecanoo Mansion London

1900	1910	1930	1950	1970	2016

Albert Court entrance hall	Waterlow Court dining room	Highpoint II entrance hall	Keeling House balcony areas (drawing)	Cripps Building roof terrace

Residential Flats, Sydney Perks, 1905

Flats, Urban Houses and Cottage Homes, W. Shaw Sparrow, 1906

The Modern Flat, Yorke and Gibberd, 1937

Architectural Review #695, 1954

Copper Lane co-housing (2009–2014)

'THE BLINDED MAN SEES WITH HIS EARS AND HANDS' MODES OF DWELLING

Simon Henley

All too often discussions about building dwell on the technocratic and formal, and the extent to which material decoration has re-emerged as a necessary dimension of all kinds of architecture, not least the domestic. But these global addictions belie a lack of purpose and content. Not so the work of the practitioners teaching at the Mackintosh School of Architecture. Instead their thoughts and work address what it means to inhabit a dwelling, and to observe that inhabitation, often at the threshold between inside and out. Studio KAP's 'Corrections' by their very nature act on, and remake, the edges of domestic space; Elder & Cannon's work enjoys the 'paraphernalia of life' to be found, and the rich experience to be had, within these threshold spaces; Stacey Philips also writes about the edges of their buildings, of 'a graduation of defined thresholds', and these spaces where they are adopted serve as a 'calm background for life'; whereas DO Architecture consider the functional-behavioural aspects of these types of space and their metrics. cameronwebster write about 'instinct' (Aalto), 'ordinariness' (Smithsons) and 'touching the senses'. Orkidstudio remind us of the absolute necessity, the economics and ethics of shelter. Ideas about culture, climate and typology recur. And Ian Alexander and Henry McKeown relate these themes to what they term the 'undesigned'. Again, and again, the notion of psycho-social and physiological space prevails.

In his poem 'Recalling War' Robert Graves wrote the lines 'The blinded man sees with his ears and hands / As much or more than once with both his eyes'.

Conference centre and offices for charity We Are 336, competition, 1st place (2008)

I first came across this when working on a competition that the practice subsequently won to adapt a Brutalist warehouse for a charity called We Are 336 that provides conference spaces and workspaces for a number of disability and age-related charities. Graves' notion was that soldiers confronted with the loss of a sense, in this case sight, might develop greater acuity in another.

In the UK, the Building Regulations and British Standards dictate how we build for disability. People talk of inclusive design and barrier-free access when describing what is expected of a design. In most cases this translates into the use of lifts and ramps, and finishes with contrasting surface tonalities (Light Reflectance Values) so that a partially sighted individual can distinguish between the floor and wall planes, and a door within a wall. These are necessary prescriptions. They are quantitative not qualitative, designed not to enrich only to enable. But Graves' words raise a much more profound point for architects and their architecture which is usually evaluated by sight, and as a consequence by our desire to judge shape and form, and indeed space by eye. His words direct us to think about the other senses – to touch, hearing, smell and taste – and about the way space works in terms of experience, not simply something to be glanced at.

For We Are 336 his words led us to propose an architecture of contrasting natural luminosities, of material textures and temperatures due to their conductivity or insulating properties, and to consider the extent to which an open window, and outside a window box or a garden terrace may bring first flora then fauna, first smells then sound, close to somebody's work or a meeting. Birdsong or the noise generated by the frequency of an insect's wings become a part of the architecture. After more than a decade this project has yet to be realized, but we are again exploring the same concerns with a project for The Poppy Factory, a charity that both employs veterans with disabilities and coaches them back to work.

'Poppy Portico', The Poppy Factory, in collaboration with artist Paul Morrison (2017–2021)

From the outset, our architecture has exploited the outdoor space adjacent to a building. The decks at Talkback framed a garden of herbs that may be crushed underfoot by staff moving between buildings created within what was, in effect, a multistorey cloister. There, the office and the idea of work were associated not with the interior but with the captured landscape. Our competition for Letchworth Town Hall envisaged the council chamber and committee rooms surrounded by a brim (much like that of a hat) that would afford shelter to those outside and at the same time give them the opportunity to be in proximity to an open window, to hear discussion and debate, and so to be closer to the democratic process.

These works suggest that it is the threshold – the morphology and fabric of the façade and space immediately beyond it – itself that becomes the architecture, the nature of which differs one from the next. A study of the threshold becomes therefore a study in type. In the case of the dwelling, the significance of the threshold lies in its capacity to associate the household with, and disassociate it from, the city; and the way in which it might establish common ground between neighbours, and within an urban quarter, all of which depend on the sensory properties of these external environments.

Letchworth Town Hall, 'Designs on Democracy' competition, 2nd place (2002)

Façade study model, Arnold Road (2016–to date)

More recently our work has turned to housing and the question of *dwelling* in liminal space. Arnold Road is a quiet street in the East End of London with railway arches on one side and a community centre on the other. Our project replaces the community centre on its triangular site between the street and an Underground line that resurfaces here. The parti breaks what might have been one long block (that would have cast long shadows) into two heavy masonry buildings surrounded by inter-connecting courtyards and gardens which are shaped by the structures. These offer sanctuary to the families that live here and a playful world for children. The arrangement permits morning and afternoon light to perme-ate between the buildings, penetrate the courtyards and illuminate the interi-ors. Each dwelling is conceived as a courtyard house, stacked one on top of another. A loggia extends the space of the hall, creating a focus for the home, and in the larger dwellings divides living rooms and bedrooms much like the floors of a house. Windows are concen-trated around the loggia, so the life of the interior is channelled through this point in the façade. The external room appears as a cleft in the masonry, its floor a small concrete bridge spanning the void, surrounded by a curtain of glass that recedes into the shadows. This protects the interiors from the noise of the trains and the impact of the sun, but also mediates between the private realm and its exposure to the metropolis.

Tent Street, another social housing scheme in London's East End, develops a different idea, the opportunity for casual association en route to a dwell-ing. Near Whitechapel, the land is isolated from the city at-large by railway lines, a housing estate and industrial compounds. Therefore any hope of urban continuity is frustrated by the sur-roundings. The design therefore has more in common with the isolated indus-trial urban artefacts to be found in the Potteries and in the Liverpool docks that ape the urbanism from which they were removed. A mews is flanked by maisonettes in a 4-storey terrace to the south and a 10-storey one to the north. Like an 18th Century new model village the design envisages a fragment of the city. Bull-nose corners mark the start of a pedestrian space, lined by front doors, bay windows and, behind these, kitchen tables. Overhead lights, suspended between the façades literally tie the buildings on either side of the precinct together. All the dwell-ings except for the lateral flats behind the bullnose are two storeys high. Those above ground are served by wide inter-nal staircases that open onto decks on every other floor. The second-floor decks project from the façade so those who use them are *in* the space, inti-mately connected to the theatre of life and the conversation below.

Mews flanked by four- and ten-storey terraces, Tent Street (2016)

Detail of dwelling framed by a pair of masonry buttresses, Tent Street (2016)

Above, where the decks are further from the ground, they recede into the body of the building. Each dwelling is framed by a pair of masonry buttresses between which the vaulted concrete walkways span. Inside this truncated but open two-storey room the dwelling and a constellation of apertures – entrance doorway, kitchen window, and above the projecting bay of the living room terrace – begin to reveal a domestic interior. Neighbours passing through this outer room – a structural and spatial distillation of the dwelling as a whole – to reach their home are incidentally passing through the domain of another household. The benches beneath the kitchen window and recessed doorway structure encounter and, when not used as such, leave traces of inhabitation. Furthermore, the living room terrace on the upper floor of the dwelling enables a resident and their neighbour to enjoy both the privacy and the theatre that this vertical arrangement allows. By contrast to the communality that the mews and first-floor deck afford, these spaces favour the more intimate association of a handful of households and at the same time a particular household's perception of the wider city. With both the Arnold Road and Tent Street social housing projects, the architecture establishes a parity between the interior and the world outside.

Like Tent Street our buildings on the post-war Frampton Park estate in Hackney take their cue from history. Both establish the dialectic between two types of construction and two kinds of space. The design for Taylor & Chatto Courts proposes three villas. Each couples a masonry block with an exposed concrete frame. Whilst not equal in area the masonry blocks and the structural frames offer parity even in the UK climate between a life lived indoors and one lived outside.

By convention each home must have private outside space. Couple this with external circulation and these two functions generate a critical mass of outside space and the opportunity to invest meaning in a frame where individuals are exposed to the more varied sensations of the natural world. Again, these frames serve as a threshold between city street and private dwelling. And there is playfulness in the way the design uses a balcony to create an entrance canopy and – saving a lift and stairs – bridges to connect the dwellings within one villa to the circulation in another. Of course, these decisions have formal implications but above all they are experiential and revitalising. In contrast to the three villas, Wilmott Court forms a small urban block or palazzo. This time the frames that wrap around the surface of the masonry block vary in depth in

Study models of Taylor, Chatto & Wilmott Court, Frampton Park Estate (2013–2021)

response to orientation and quiet or busy thoroughfares, to lesson the impact of street life on the interior.

At a much larger scale, the 400 homes of the Nightingale Estate create a new urban quarter. Our design[1] establishes a number of new north-south streets. Oriel windows project the domestic interiors of east- and west-facing dual-aspect apartments out into the space of the street. Common entrances and passageways connect street and communal garden. Each terrace of the apartments forms a belvedere – the gable end façade – overlooking Hackney Downs. The proposition offers the prospect of a model district where the specific architecture, like much of that of the 18th- and 19th-century city, plays only a supporting role. Compare these situations and sensations, the conscious product of restraint, to the cacophony of scales and forms that do little more than signify the value of property and in so doing continue to fragment the city fabric.

Co-housing is different. Residents share activities such as childcare and gardening. The social and economic imperatives mean the architect must explore where to draw the line, the threshold, between one household and their neighbours, the home and the city. What most of us think of as home seeps out into the communal spaces – where we eat, where we wash our cloths, mend the bike, where children play, and how and where we exercise. Communal meals and gardening naturally create social patterns for residents of all ages. And in an inter-generational community the old may look after the young.

The residents of Copper Lane describe how their 'project developed out of a shared interest in a way of living that would allow [them] as a group to have more interaction with each other

than in regular terraced houses which typically come with private gardens and a sense that the public sphere ends at the front door.' The alienating effects of modern life encouraged them to pursue a more communal approach that would provide companionship and mutual support.

The six households share a continuous perimeter of communal gardens which offer varied atmospheres, and inside a laundry, workshop and hall – for exercise classes, parties and communal projects. The design develops a typology that manifests the idea of 'communality'. The resulting cluster model places a court at the heart of the back land site beneath which the communal facilities are located and around which the houses are planned. Two two-storey houses are located east and west of the hall, the four three-storey houses to the north and south, thereby reconciling the discrepancy between the orientation of the site and the path of the sun.

The lower ground floor is submerged 1.2 metres below ground, bringing the window cills and the expansive sliding windows down to earth, and the flora and fauna outside to chest level. Each house is unique, the internal arrangement of spaces, window positions and dimensions and cill heights negotiating the exposure to both the elements and neighbouring folk, and the privacy of each dwelling, each room within each dwelling even, in particular around the central court. The rough timber and masonry surfaces complete an environment that may be seen, touched, heard, smelled and, from time to time, tasted. Overall, the sharing of the qualities of the site is a negotiated form of egalitarianism.

1   The design is a collaboration with Stephen Taylor Architects and Karakusevic Carson Architects

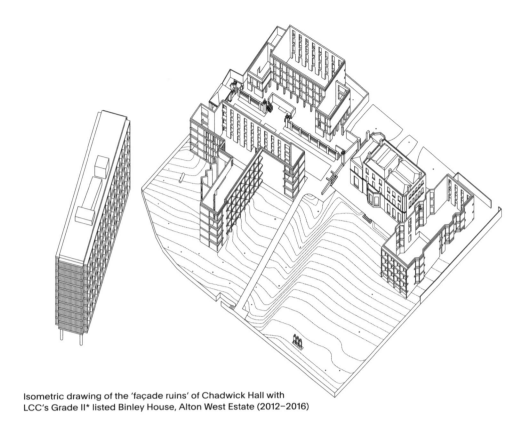

Isometric drawing of the 'façade ruins' of Chadwick Hall with
LCC's Grade II* listed Binley House, Alton West Estate (2012–2016)

By comparison to co-housing and contemporary social housing, student accommodation with its minimal floorspace and access to natural light and air is often an extreme form of the *Existenzminimum*. Chadwick Hall at Roehampton University seeks to remedy this phenomenon. Here, students live in a mix of flats and houses in three buildings set within the gardens of a Georgian villa on the edge of the London County Council's[2] Brutalist Alton West Estate – itself the appropriation of 18th-century parkland. Each of the buildings employs a distinct plan type, and two are paired around an existing sunken garden to form a new court. Communal rooms are carefully positioned in relation to the type and siting of each building. But it is their construction that distinguishes these dwellings. The vice-chancellor sought an intentionally theatrical relationship between the student rooms and the outside world. As a result, every student in every room – or *camera* – has a balcony, the door to which serves as the aperture to the landscape. The construction encases conventional, concrete-framed structures inside free-standing, loadbearing brick and pre-cast-concrete structures. The interiors are therefore wrapped in heavy 'ruins', with deep walls that incorporate these balconies mediating between the common ground of the remarkable landscape enjoyed by all and the more private realm of the individual student's room. The sentient student is caste into the roles of both actor and receptor.

These works explore and exploit liminal space and the connection between on the one hand typology, structure and

2   The adjacent slab and point blocks were designed
    by Bill Howell, John Killick, John Partridge and Stan
    Amis while working at the London County Council

matter and on the other pyscho-social and physiological phenomena. Contemporary buildings can and should point to a strong public life and a commitment to social values, and to an architecture of social solidarity and individual perception. It is by these means and not the more prevalent obsession with hyperbolic forms and material decoration – a symptom of our materialist culture – deployed in the design of dwellings, judged by eye, often from a photograph, that will serve as the durable foundations for a community. As Graves reminds us in 'Recalling War', it is the possibility that 'the blinded man sees with his ears and hands' that directs our practice to think about the other senses – touch, hearing, smell and taste – and to the way space works in terms of experience.

Chadwick Hall (2012–2016)

DWELLING-ON LESSONS AND PRACTICES IN ARCHITECTURE

Graeme Hutton

Ruminations on dwelling abound – a rabbit hole, while doubtless a cosy dwelling for the rabbit, is none the less a potentially disorienting theme to attach meaning to in determining buildings as good architecture. Indeed, dwelling as a theme is often used as the beginning of an architectural education. The assumption being that it is an appropriate level as a starter project rooted in lived experience, yet in the early years students are only learning how to live and to frame their values as independents. The most abstract and detached or empty designs produced are anticipated by tutors with overwrought briefs (the one-legged tie collector was a wry observation of Isi Metzstein) to gift and predetermine a kind of ersatz specificity. Living space in itself (not the same as dwelling, of course) has certain advantages for the teacher, however, in that it is normative enough to use as a conceit, to teach more generic lessons around plan/section/form and introduce wider ideas around typology.

So what are the common architectural observations on dwelling evident in the designs and texts of the pracademics in this volume? How might we speculate and interpret these concerns as they inform the fundamental lessons of/for architecture?

The first and very obvious shared concern is the motivation to both practise and teach. Often, seasoned practitioners approach Schools of Architecture with an earnest desire to 'give something back' – this 'something' is not always well defined or indeed evident in an often extensive body of work. What characterises the most interesting teachers is an underlying doubt – where they seek to gain something from teaching – to test and question their received wisdom outside the commercial constraints (or excuses) which condition private practice, and the production of *projets manque*. That is to say projects which, although critically regarded by the cognoscenti, are fated to never fulfil the elusive ideal ambition of the architect. Rarely, if ever, is a real building a fully realised idea.

This volume, in a way, gives space to this doubt by demanding a higher level of discourse than the merely descriptive from the contributing architects. It is interesting to observe how the collected architects/teachers use design/writing as a means to articulate positions regarding design process and object. Positions that are at once personal and also speculative on architecture's wider impact.

Architecture and architectural design processes are often described here in terms of reconciled dualities: science and art, form and function, facts and feelings, tradition and modernity, path and place, structure and construction, served and servant, and so on. Used intelligently these dualities can be skilfully manipulated and synthesised to create architectural works that are not simply new buildings, but may be thought of as articulating genuinely 'new knowledge'. The practice-based teachers here find common ground, perhaps unknowingly, in that they all engage with notions of the dialectic in architecture as both a conceptual driver and a critical tool in both the conception and the reception of their buildings.

The dialectic is interpreted for the purposes of this text as Chalybaus's original reading of Hegel as 'Thesis–Antitheses–Synthesis'. It is a generic logic system within which an architect consistently works – it superscribes a body of work. It is the original Hegelian tripartite articulations of this system, framed as 'Abstract–Negative–Concrete' (*The Phenomenology of Mind*, Hegel, 1807) which, by my reading, shape and form the individual designs and supporting texts presented in this volume. As a self-imposed critical framework it is a useful device to problem form in both design practice and the teaching studio.

Problem forming is of course the very foundation of innovation – if innovation, as practitioners and teachers, is indeed what we seek. This raises wider questions in architectural education (which in itself is a form of dialectic) central to which is reconciling the relationship – tension even – between education and training. The tutor/pupil engagement oscillates between amanuensis and muse. At its best the concerns of the thoughtful practitioner/teacher will propel a studio to new insights, while not losing sight of the fact that architecture has craft at its core. We are predominantly concerned with buildings as things, things which have the capacity to resonate with us in all sorts of sensory ways. Paul Williams captured this nicely in response to Deyan Sudjic's critical framing of the new Design Museum as '… a museum of ideas rather than things'. 'Well, I thought …,' Williams responded, '… if I'm inspired and engaged, what more could I ask for? The only niggle I had was Sudjic's implied suppression of "things" – I like to encounter "things". I like "things" that are aesthetically pleasing and challenging, whether high-end or ordinary and every-day. I want to be moved by what I see as well as what I read and to be provoked by the tangible as well

as the intangible' (*Architecture Today*, No. 274, Jan. 2017). This, it might be argued, is both a metaphor for a proper architectural education, and the reason for this publication.

The works presented here can be classified in a number of ways. The most obvious of these is scale, or more accurately, size. In dealing with the issue of scale/size Kenneth Frampton provides a useful framework through which to measure the success (or otherwise) of a work of architecture. At the Docomomo conference in Barcelona in the early 90s, he was discussing 'megaforms' saying that '… good architecture should work at three levels – distant, intermediate & intimate …' (from my recollection). This has remained a critical touchstone. It is both precise and yet elastic in its ability to accommodate a critical discourse from the city to the door handle – a range evident in the buildings and critical writings in this volume. What is important is that, regardless of the scale of dialectic examined, the end point, the 'synthesis', is artfully realised as an arguable communion of oppositions.

From modest domestic extensions through single to collective dwellings, the primary opposition of individual/collective is variously articulated as '… privacy and togetherness' Chris Platt, Studio KAP; '… sheltered and cosy …larger and more open …' cameronwebster (intimate); '… privacy and neighbourliness' Adrian Stewart, DO Architecture; '… anonymous and communal' Stacey Phillips, Gordon Murray Architects (intermediate); and '… protected family intimacy on the finest threshold of the civic realm' Stephen Hoey, Elder & Cannon (distant). Although sharing the same root concern, the architectural tropes employed recognise notions of dwelling according to occupation, scale and context. It is in plan and section that the reconciliation of intimate concerns is most keenly experienced.

Studio KAP's Braefoot has some advantage here in inheriting given constraints – the existing thick-walled/small-opening traditional cottage providing a ready foil from which to spring a more transparent two-storey addition of stacked rooms. A figured dégagement mediates between old and new. It is a small core which simultaneously references Philip Johnson's 'Glass House' and Aalto's Villa Mairea – there's an opposition to contend with. What characterises Studio KAP's projects is not in fact a true reconciliation of the dialectic. The work recognises a host of oppositions and skilfully disperses them in reorganised plan and section arrangements – the oppositions are carefully controlled. Platt himself references Kahn's idea of 'a society of rooms' and this notion extends to a formal realisation where new elements confidently present their own identity as little buildings on their own terms. This is partly a product of phased adaptation and partly a carefully crafted idea around dwelling as an intimate interpretation of how their clients wish to live. The supporting text positions the architect quietly in this process. Seemingly selfless and without ego, it is an architecture which allows clients to know themselves better though the process of making a building. It is not a stretch to suggest that in this the architect is operating as a teacher, drawing out the right questions and allowing clients to problem-form, learn and co-develop solutions centred on how they choose to dwell.

Similar in programme and scale, cameronwebster's architecture embraces equally intimate concerns. What differentiates them, however, is a process driven by an almost Venturi-like enjoyment of the possibilities offered by engagement with the dialectic at multiple levels of both thought and deed. Their methods are reminiscent of the composer and teacher Hans Henze's (paraphrased) reflections when asked how he develops a composition – '... very much like I imagine an architect designs a building ...' he commented. 'First I have a sense of the whole piece, and then lots of smaller ideas enter in to build it, some of which don't fit, and so I set them aside for use later in other projects.' It is cameronwebster's 'Will to Artfulness' that is the overriding concern here. Formed through an interplay of the tacit and the technical they desire buildings 'with an edge' – sharp and formed in a Miesian sense yet contextual and cosy where appropriate. It is a difficult balancing act that is tested through drawing and modelling against the polar positions of 'Ordinariness and Light' at a theoretical level, and more visceral phenomenological oppositions such as big and small, transparent and solid towards an architecture with a rational yet poetic autonomy. These intellectual concerns predispose cameronwebster to think beyond the relative immediacy of client need in the here and now. They recognise the characteristics and specificity of dwelling as a type whose generic lessons may be further applied and developed in later compositions. In this they demonstrate a trajectory of maturing work that is the hallmark of the reflective practitioner/teacher.

Occupying a more difficult intermediate 'liminal space' are DO Architecture (Adrian Stewart) and Gordon Murray Architects (Stacey Phillips). While the dialectic remains a creative muse it is taken literally outside the formal envelope of the individual family dwelling to the shared access spaces where preoccupations of privacy and neighbourliness are architecturally determined in pursuit of community –

community in terms of social engagement and community in terms of architectural expression. A socio-urban contextual responsibility where the buildings belong to us all as part of the fabric of our dwelling in the city.

The architecture of these works is less passive than the individual family dwelling. It is described in both texts as having the capacity to be an active agent in predetermining desired collective behaviours. Typologically the buildings are different; one a composition of clustered mid-rise towers paired around shared access stairs (Gordon Murray Architects), the other a dual aspect mid-rise block with shared 'deck access' (DO). Both, however, recognise an idea of the shared space as a 'room' which can, by architectural means, suggest/allow both private and communal use. DO have the biggest challenge here and, through careful research, construct an idea about thresholds – both parallel and perpendicular to the main body of the building. It is this latter move which is the most interesting. To envisage a continuous deck as a kind of enfilade of phenomenal thresholds between implied 'rooms'.

These important 'rooms' in both works are given definition by part-screened enclosure and careful attention to detail at an intimate level. In thematically grouping these two works one is reminded of Michiel Brinkman's Justus van Effen as an imagined hybrid between them – one which might better address and resolve the architectural opportunities offered by confronting individual and collective expression as a more intermediate, innovative urban-scaled formal proposition.

This kind of associative thought, between the room and the city, between community and privacy, and between detail and experiencing architecture, is a useful construct in teaching practice and it finds itself here in the constructed narrative around which Elder & Cannon (Stephen Hoey) read a history of types as the genesis of their work. The city as teacher is writ large in the confident architecture and rich supporting text – the latter as crafted and wrought as the buildings themselves. There are no fashionable architectural tricks and tropes in the work and the text is a-temporal in this regard, positioning the work as an aggregation of historic moments as defined through the architectural experience of the city dweller. To dwell, for these architects, is a cornucopia of lived experience, framed – perhaps orchestrated – through their architecture. A defining strength of which is that, although recently constructed, it already projects a sense of history and well-lived-in permanence.

Continuity and inventiveness is opposition at play here. Or at its more basic, the interplay of tradition and modernity, where tradition is rooted finally here in vernacularity. Both jmarchitects (McKeown and Alexander) and Orkidstudio (James Mitchell) frame their work in this context. To the former the signals of dwelling are figurative elements to be commodified and abstracted; 'gables, profiles, chimneys, snoods and projections' form a taxonomy of dwelling. Their abstraction and replay provide opportunities to recognise both collective composition (the terrace) and individual expression in reconciling what Venturi terms '… the difficult whole' (Robert Venturi, *Complexity and Contradiction in Architecture*, MoMA, 1977, p. 88). This is of course an interest in an artful play with vernacular form, designed to suggest the continuity of architecture as represented by an aggregation of deeply known object motifs – themselves dwelling in relation to the particularities of a given place.

The vernacular and its abstraction is, in our contemporary context, a conceit. It is a device or self-imposed intellectual constraint in an otherwise open intellectual playing field. Of course, it might be argued that without constraints we have no culture, and that the tougher the actual constraints the more authentic any response must strive to be. In this context it is Orkidstudio who most closely approach Heidegger. Their text, largely descriptive of process, makes no mention of 'dwelling' and yet it is riven with it – a core idea centred around teaching a community skills towards an architecture based on the modest desire for '… place-making and comfort …'. The architecture that results is so far from utilitarian building in its understanding, embodiment and formal expression of a culture – legibly communicating the act of its making and breathing the same air as its inhabitants.

Their work forcefully reminds us that the act of building is dwelling – and this is ultimately and always a fundamental lesson in creating building as dwelling.

BIOGRAPHIES

CHRISTOPHER PLATT

is co-founder of Studio KAP architects and Chair of Architecture at the Mackintosh School of Architecture, where he was previously Head of School. His first 20 years of architectural practice were spent in Glasgow, London, Oxford, Ethiopia and Berlin, followed by 20 years combining teaching and practice-based research in academia with critical, reflective practice in Studio KAP exploring the creative reciprocity between concepts and details, figures and grounds, old and new, both in Global North and Global South contexts.

DICK VAN GAMEREN

is Professor of housing design and Dean of the Faculty of Architecture and the Built Environment, TUDelft, Netherlands. He is founding editor of the book series *DASH, Delft Architectural Studies on Housing*. He is currently developing the Global Housing Study Centre for research and education on affordable housing in the Global South. He is also a practising architect and partner of MecanooArchitecten. In 2007 he received an Aga Khan Award, and in 2012 the Best Building of the Year Award of the Dutch Association of Architects.

SIMON HENLEY

is a principal of London-based architecture studio Henley Halebrown, who were shortlisted for the Stirling Prize in 2018. Simon studied at the University of Liverpool. He combines practice with teaching, writing and research, and is the author of *The Architecture of Parking* (Thames & Hudson, 2007) and *Redefining Brutalism* (RIBA Publications, 2017). Simon is a postgraduate unit master at the Kingston School of Art where he is also undertaking a PhD by Practice. In 2018 Swiss publishers Quart Verlag published a monograph on Henley Halebrown in their De Aedibus International series.

GRAEME HUTTON

is Professor of Architecture and Associate Dean of Learning and Teaching at the University of Dundee. He is an architect who has been engaged in practice and education for over 20 years. Working with Dundee's LJR+H Chartered Architects, his designs have been widely exhibited, including at the Venice Biennale of Architecture and Royal Academy. 'Drummond House–The Shed' has won numerous architectural awards, including a 2009 RIBA Award. It has been published internationally in the professional and popular press, including *The New York Times*. The recently completed 'Zinc-House' was longlisted for the RIBA/Grand Designs 'House of the Year 2016' award and was filmed by Channel 4 for broadcast in November 2016. Graeme was elected an 'Academician' of The Royal Scottish Academy in 2016. As a Masters Unit teacher he continues to use the City of Dundee as a context to explore the potential of architecture as an agent of social and cultural transformation.

JAMES MITCHELL

co-founded BuildX Studio in 2016 and its predecessor, Orkidstudio, in 2008. A trained architect living in Nairobi, in 2016 he was named in Impact Design Hub's '40 under 40' and in 2018 was selected as an Aspen Institute Spotlight Health Fellow. James has also gone on to create Buildher, a construction skills training programme for disadvantaged women in Kenya. He was a design tutor at the Mackintosh School of Architecture from 2013 to 2016.

MIRANDA WEBSTER

is an architect, teacher and researcher, dividing her time between cameron-webster architects, and teaching at the Mackintosh School of Architecture. Her practice harnesses tactics developed within research in academia and in the studio, to pursue architectural interests in the use of drawing as a speculative tool and as a way of understanding building processes.

HENRY MCKEOWN & IAN ALEXANDER

have been design tutors at the Mackintosh School of Architecture for almost 30 years. They have also taught in Edinburgh, Aberdeen, London and Belfast. They are also practising architects, formerly as McKeown Alexander and currently jmarchitects. Their work has been shortlisted for the Mies van der Rohe Award and has received numerous awards, including at the RIBA Awards, Civic Trust Awards, GIA Awards, Saltire Awards and Scottish Design Awards. The work has been exhibited in New York, Rotterdam, Paris, London and Edinburgh. Recently the practice has worked with Steven Holl Architects of New York on the Glasgow School of Art Reid Building and a new Maggie's Centre at St Bartholomew's Hospital in London. Henry has an interest in tiny drawings and paintings which encapsulate the essence of architectural ideas in his work. Ian has an interest in drawings and paintings which record architectural forms and volumes, which in turn inform his own architectural explorations and work.

STACEY PHILLIPS

is an architect living and working in Glasgow with a keen interest in how people occupy and personalise space. Stacey worked on Telford Drive while a project director at Gordon Murray Architects and is now an Associate Partner with Sheppard Robson Architects in their Glasgow office. She is currently a final year design tutor at the Mackintosh School of Architecture.

ADRIAN STEWART

is Director of DO Architecture (www.do-architecture.co.uk) and a studio tutor and lecturer at the Mackintosh School of Architecture at the Glasgow School of Art. He is interested in collaboration across the disciplines and experimentation in the design process, often using light. He is also a Certified Passive House Designer. He has worked on projects across the UK and Europe, including i360 in Brighton with Marks Barfield Architects, and in 2012 represented Scotland at the Venice Biennale of Architecture, for which he was jointly awarded the RSA Gold Medal.

STEPHEN HOEY

graduated from the Mackintosh School of Architecture in 1995 and received a number of awards throughout his student career, most notably the RIBA Bronze Medal and the RIBA Serjeant Award for Drawing. After a period of extended study in the Barcelona studio of Enrique Miralles he returned to Glasgow where he worked with Elder & Cannon from 1996 to 2020. The practice was established in 1982 by Tom Elder and Dick Cannon and has consistently achieved recognition at a national level throughout its 45-year history, including a number of RIBA Awards and the honour of being awarded the RIAS Doolan Award for 'Best Building in Scotland' on three separate occasions. In 2008 Stephen adopted the role of Design Director in the practice while continuing his role as Design Tutor at The Mack, both roles linked by his continued practice on a number of residential, educational, commercial and public projects in the urban centre of the City of Glasgow.

IMAGE CREDITS

Andrew Lee Photography: 55, 97, 84,
    87 bottom, 89, 97 bottom, 100, 101, 103
Cameronwebster: 50, 54, 56 middle
    and bottom, 57 middle and bottom,
    59, 60, 61
Christopher Platt: 38 top
Dapple Photography: 52–53, 56 top, 60
David Grandorge: 141
David Robert Barbour: 148
Dick van Gameren: 138–139
DO Architecture: 94, 97, 98, 99, 102
Elder & Cannon: 107, 108 top, 109 bottom,
    111, 112, 113 top right, 116, 118 top right,
    119, 120, 122, 123, 124, 125
Henley Halebrown: 142, 143,
    144 top left, 146
Henry McKeown: 64, 70 bottom
Jim Stevenson: 147
JM architects: 66, 67, 68, 69, 70, 72,
    73, 75, 76, 79
Ian Alexander: 65, 68, 69, 71, 73, 78
Keith Hunter Photography: 10, 12, 35,
    36 top, 37 top right and bottom right,
    42 top, 45 top, 46, 47, 57, 58, 108,
    110, 114–115
Martin Philimore Photography: 59
Nick Kane: 140
Odysseas Mourtzouchos: 22, 23, 24 top
Orkidstudio: 16, 20, 25, 26, 27 bottom
Peter Dibdin: 18–19, 21
Sean Deckert: 74
Stacey Philips / Gordon Murray
    Architects: 82, 83, 87, 90–91
Ståle Eriksen: 144 bottom right
Stephen Doherty / Gordon Murray
    Architects: 83
Studio Kap: 30, 31, 32, 33, 34,
    38 bottom, 39, 42 bottom,
    45 bottom left
Cover sketch: Stacey Phillips

INDEX

Abstraction 77, 133, 137, 152, 153
Adaptation 31, 39, 151
Adrian Stewart 9, 95, 150, 151
Affordability (housing) 25, 26, 96, 133, 134, 137
Agrarian architecture 32, 70
Aldo Rossi 70, 77
Alienation 136, 145
Alison and Peter Smithson 51, 141
Alterations 33, 39, 44, 45
Alton West Estate 146
Alvar Aalto 51, 61, 86,
Anonymity 85, 103, 136, 150
Architect (role of) 11, 13, 26, 43, 47, 51, 61, 73, 85, 88, 95, 133, 135, 136, 145, 149, 151
Architectural education (also teaching) 13, 141, 149, 150, 152
Authority (housing) 83, 85, 87, 136
Author 13, 65, 73, 85

Beaux Arts 61
Belonging 83, 85, 88, 102
Bergpolder Flat 135
Binley House 146
Blackhouse 66, 67, 69, 72, 77, 78, 136
Braefoot 151, 32, 34, 48
British Arts and Crafts 133
Brutalism 135, 141, 146
Building regulations 95, 141
Bungalow 39, 40, 41

Cameronwebster 51, 136, 141, 150, 151
Caricaturisation 133
César Pelli 32, 33
Chadwick Hall 146, 147
Children's home 22, 23, 25
Christopher Platt 31, 150, 151
Chittagong University 17
CIAM 135
Circulation (also movement patterns) 61, 96, 98, 99, 102, 136, 144
Cityscape 137
Client 36, 43, 47, 51, 61, 95, 151
Climate (also micro-climate) 54, 56, 59, 70, 111, 124, 136, 141, 144
Cluster 32, 145, 152
Co-housing 140, 145, 146

Collaboration 43, 47, 73, 77, 135
Collective housing 68, 134, 135, 138, 139, 150
Commission 47
Community (togetherness) 13, 83, 86, 95, 102, 103, 145, 146, 147, 151, 152, 153
Conservation 43, 47, 136
Context (cultural, historic, spatial) 13, 41, 43, 47, 69, 70, 77, 85, 119, 136, 137, 150, 151, 152, 153
Continuity 35, 133, 143, 152
Continuity of methods 133
Corrections (spatial, compositional) 31, 44, 47, 141
Covid-19 11, 13
Cross ventilation 98
Culture (also cultural change) 83, 141, 153
Customs and traditions 137

Daylight 32, 37, 44, 54, 96, 98, 102
Deck (also open access deck and terrace) 38, 54, 86, 88, 91, 95, 96, 98, 102, 103, 124, 142, 152
Density 65, 95, 96, 98, 103
Detailing (and ornament) 70, 88, 135
Dick van Gameren 9, 133
Disability 141
Discourse (architectural) 149, 150
Divis Flats 103
DO Architecture 95, 136, 141, 150, 151
Docomomo 150
Drawing (technique) 61, 71, 73, 78, 151
Dwelling 11, 13, 38, 39, 43, 47, 65, 68, 73, 88, 95, 98, 107, 111, 124, 135, 141, 142, 143, 144, 145, 146, 147, 149, 150, 151, 152, 153

Earthbags 20, 25, 26
Egalitarianism 145
Elder & Cannon 137, 150, 152
Everyday life 13, 47, 83, 85, 124, 137
Evolution 31, 39, 133
Existenzminimum 135, 146
Expression (architectural, formal) 85, 88, 152, 153
Expression (personal) 85, 87, 124, 136, 152

Family 13, 20, 39, 44, 45, 47, 83,
    124, 135, 150, 151, 152
Flora and fauna 111, 142, 145
Formalism 51
Frampton Park Estate 144

Gallery (also gallery access) 61, 135,
    138, 143, 144
Garden (gardening) 11, 39, 40, 45,
    49, 54, 59, 68, 85, 86, 90, 91, 99,
    135, 142, 145, 146
Geometry 36, 119
Gerrit Rietveld 135
Giorgio Grassi 70
Glass House 151
Gordon Murray Architects 83, 136,
    150, 152
Govanhill, South Glasgow 95, 96, 136
Graeme Hutton 9, 149
Grameen Bank 20

Hans Henze 151
Hellen's House 17, 20, 25, 26, 27, 137
Hellen Nyambura Kamau 20, 21,
    24, 25, 26
Henry McKeown 9, 65, 141, 152
High-rise 135
History (and historic) 70, 77, 103,
    119, 133, 144, 152
Home (concept of) 25, 26, 27, 39,
    44, 47, 86, 88, 96, 124, 145
Household 17, 20, 142, 144, 145

Ian Alexander 9, 65, 141, 152
Ideal standard 135,
Identity 13, 83, 96, 124, 151
Imitation 133, 137
Inclusive design 141
Individuality (individualism) 13, 68,
    83, 85, 88, 136, 147, 150, 152
Innovation 133, 134, 137, 150
Interior (domestic) 31, 78, 142,
    143, 144, 145, 146
Isi Metzstein 149
Italianism 70
Italian neo-rationalists 70, 77

Jacob Bakema 135, 136
James Mitchell 9, 17, 152
Jmarchitects 65, 136, 152
Johannes van den Broek 135

Juhani Pallasmaa 85
Justus van Effen Complex 152

Kenneth Frampton 150
Kevin Roche 47

Landscape 32, 36, 38, 59, 60,
    77, 78, 86, 90, 96, 119, 136, 137,
    142, 146
Laurieston project 119, 137
Le Corbusier 135
Letchworth Town Hall 142
Lifestyle 26, 54, 133
London County Council 146
Long Gallery House 32
Louis Kahn 39, 151
Lunga 54, 56, 59, 63

Mabati roof 26
Mackay Hugh Baillie Scott 133
Mackintosh School of Architecture
    70, 141
Magnification 133
Manor Estates Housing
    Association 83
Martin Heidegger 153
Massing 39, 88, 96
Materials (selection of, palette)
    17, 26, 35, 83, 86, 88, 111, 137, 142
Medieval 137
Micro-finance 25
Michiel Brinkman 152
Miesian (style) 151
Mini-society 39
Miranda Webster 9, 51
Model (architectural) 60, 61, 69,
    95, 135, 136, 143, 144, 151
Modernism 135
Monotony 135
Morphology 111, 142
Muhammad Yunus 17, 20

Neighbours (neighbourliness)
    83, 86, 87, 88, 96, 98, 102, 103,
    142, 144, 145, 146, 150, 151
Neighbourhood (urban quarter)
    111, 142, 145
Nightingale Estate 145
North Gardner Street 54, 62

Oakley Drive 39, 49
Orkidstudio 17, 20, 137, 141, 152, 153
Ownership 68, 83, 86, 96, 102, 103

Park Hill Housing 103, 136
Past and present 133
Palazzo (and keep) 107, 124, 137, 144
Parks (and greens) 88, 96, 135, 146
Perimeter block 135,
Permanence 31, 152
Peter Buchanan 77
Peter Zumthor 47, 61
Phenomenology 78, 150, 151
Philip Johnson 151
Phillip Moffat 88
Placemaking 96
Poppy Factory 142
Poverty 17, 25
Practice (architectural) 13, 26, 43, 78,
    149, 150
Precedents (also historic) 26, 51, 61,
    95, 96
Prefabrication 135
Principles (and methods) 33, 51, 83,
    85, 95
Privacy (private space, intimacy)
    13, 39, 44, 47, 54, 68, 83, 86, 88, 91,
    95, 96, 98, 99, 107, 124, 135, 137,
    143, 144, 145, 146, 147, 150, 151, 152
Process 11, 13, 43, 47, 61, 95, 103,
    119, 133, 142, 149, 151, 153
Programme 51, 151
Psychological impact 95, 141, 147

Regionalism 69
Registered Social Landlord 95
Resourcefulness 88
Reuse 31, 65
Robert Graves 141, 147
Robert Maguire 47
Robert Venturi 151, 152
Roehampton University 146

Security 26, 98, 124
Self-referential 77
Settlement 31, 34
Shack 20
Shelter 13, 26, 36, 47, 54, 59, 88,
    90, 141, 142, 150
Simon Henley 9, 141
Single people 133, 135

Social cohesiveness 95
Social housing 83, 85
Socializing 39, 44, 86, 90, 98,
    102, 103, 124, 142, 145
Social reform 133
Social values 147, 151
Society of rooms 39, 151
Stacey Phillips 9, 83, 141, 150, 151
St Aloysius College 107
Stealth House 69, 73, 77
Stephen Hoey 9, 107, 150, 152
Streets in the sky 98
Student housing 146, 147
Suburban 39, 135
Sustainable design 83

Tarvie Lodge 60, 61, 62
Taxonomy of dwelling 152
Taylor Court & Chatto Court 144
Team Ten 135, 136
Terrace (terraced house) 39, 40,
    41, 65, 68, 69, 73, 78, 80, 96,
    135, 136, 143, 152
Territory 39, 95, 98
Texture 35, 111, 119, 142
Timber framing 20, 26, 107
Topography 57, 111
Townhouse 65, 107
Tradition 133, 134, 135, 136, 137,
    149, 152
Typology 13, 61, 69, 73, 95, 96, 103,
    107, 111, 133, 137, 141, 145, 146, 149

Urbanism 143
Utilitarian 51, 153
Un-designed 73

Vernacular 32, 69, 70, 137, 152, 153
Victorian 96, 111
Villa Mairea 151
Vocabulary (architectural language)
    77, 136

Walter Gropius 135
Waterlow Court 133
We Are 336 141, 142
Willem van Tijen 135,
Wilmott Court 144

Zuidpleinflat 135

Imprint

Edited by: Christopher Platt
Proofreading: Dean Drake
Design: Bureau Sandra Doeller
Plans and visualisations: Ania Kozak
Pre-press image editing: Marjeta Morinc
Printing, and binding: DZA Druckerei
zu Altenburg GmbH, Thuringia

Park Books
Niederdorfstrasse 54
8001 Zurich
Switzerland
www.park-books.com

Park Books is being supported by the
Federal Office of Culture with a general
subsidy for the years 2021–2024.

ISBN 978-3-03860-238-5